Civilizations in Embrace

The **Nalanda-Sriwijaya Centre (NSC)** at the Institute of Southeast Asian Studies, Singapore, pursues research on historical interactions among Asian societies and civilizations. It serves as a forum for comprehensive study of the ways in which Asian polities and societies have interacted over time through religious, cultural, and economic exchanges and diasporic networks. The Research Series provides scholars with an avenue to present the outcome of their research and allows an opportunity to develop new or innovative approaches in the sphere of intra-Asian interactions.

The **Institute of Southeast Asian Studies (ISEAS)** was established as an autonomous organization in 1968. It is a regional centre dedicated to the study of socio-political, security and economic trends and developments in Southeast Asia and its wider geostrategic and economic environment. The Institute's research programmes are the Regional Economic Studies (RES, including ASEAN and APEC), Regional Strategic and Political Studies (RSPS), and Regional Social and Cultural Studies (RSCS).

ISEAS Publishing, an established academic press, has issued more than 2,000 books and journals. It is the largest scholarly publisher of research about Southeast Asia from within the region. ISEAS Publishing works with many other academic and trade publishers and distributors to disseminate important research and analyses from and about Southeast Asia to the rest of the world.

Civilizations in Embrace

The Spread of Ideas and the Transformation of Power

India and Southeast Asia in the Classical Age

Amitav Acharya

ISEAS

INSTITUTE OF SOUTHEAST ASIAN STUDIES
Singapore

First published in Singapore in 2013
by ISEAS Publishing
Institute of Southeast Asian Studies
30 Heng Mui Keng Terrace, Pasir Panjang
Singapore 119614
E-mail: publish@iseas.edu.sg
Website: http://bookshop.iseas.edu.sg

ISEAS Library Cataloguing-in-Publication Data

Acharya, Amitav, 1962-
   Civilizations in embrace : the spread of ideas and the transformation of power :
India and Southeast Asia in the classical age.
   1. Southeast Asia—Civilization—Indic influences.
   2. Southeast Asia—Relations—India.
   3. India—Relations—Southeast Asia.
   4. Southeast Asia—Politics and government.
   I. Title.
DS523.2 A17   2013

ISBN 978-981-4379-73-1 (hard cover)
ISBN 978-981-4379-74-8 (E-book PDF)

Cover design: Qu'est-ce Que C'est Design

Cover photo: The Golden Voyage: Traders (*Sadhavas*) from ancient Kalinga
(modern Orissa on the east coast of India) being given a ceremonial send-off by
their families on their voyage to Southeast Asian lands. Contemporary Orissan
painting, courtesy of Amitav Acharya. Photograph by Lu Caixia

Typeset by International Typesetters Pte Ltd
Printed in Singapore by Photoplates Pte Ltd

CONTENTS

FOREWORD

The name Amitav Acharya needs little introduction to those who are involved with the study of contemporary international relations in Asia. His work on Asian regionalism and particularly that which engages with Southeast Asia and ASEAN brought him initial fame, while his research on international institutions and security arrangements has seen him become even better-known. His long-time penchant for the study of non-Western modes of international relations has, however, always assumed a high prominence in his work, and this has, in recent years, been manifested in various studies including a book of the Bandung Conference and its significance for illuminating international relations in Cold War Asia.[1] While engaging with Aaron Friedberg's thesis which held that Asia is "ripe for rivalry,"[2] he has also been questioning why there is an absence of

---

[1] Tan See Seng and Amitav Acharya (eds.). *Bandung Revisited: The Legacy of the 1955 Asian-African Conference for International Order* (Singapore: Singapore University Press, 2008).

[2] For which, see Aaron L. Friedberg. "Ripe for Rivalry: Prospects for Peace in a Multipolar Asia". *International Security*, vol. 18, no. 3 (Winter 1993/94), pp. 5–33.

non-Western international relations theory.[3] Debates with scholars such as David Kang on the nature of Asian international relation through time,[4] have seen Acharya, among others, exploring how we might portray the interstate and inter-cultural relations of Asia, past and present.[5] These and other conversations led to a 2011 conference at the University of Southern California, to investigate "Was there an historical East Asian international system? Impact, meaning, and conceptualization." This brought together historians and international relations specialists to interrogate possible Asian sources for alternate international relations theory, and to examine whether indeed premodern forms of inter-state relations were different in Asia.

The volume before you is, in some ways, a continuance of the ideas explored in these earlier works by Amitav. Its title "Civilizations in Embrace" conveys the overall theme of the volume — that Asian cultures and civilisations engage with each other in ways which are communicative rather than combatative. Amitav aims through this volume to "advance the case for considering alternative models of diffusion of ideas and culture in world politics," through "one of the most extensive examples of the spread of ideas in the history of civilization; the diffusion of Indian religious and political ideas to Southeast Asia before the advent of Islam and European colonialism."

---

[3] Amitav Acharya and Barry Buzan. "Why is there no non-Western international relations theory? An introduction". *International Relations of the Asia-Pacific*, vol. 7, no. 3 (2007), pp. 287–312; and Amitav Acharya and Barry Buzan (eds.). *Non-Western International Relations Theory: Perspectives on and Beyond Asia*. London and New York: Routledge, 2010.

[4] David Kang, "Hierarchy, Balancing, and Empirical Puzzles in Asian International Relations". *International Security*, vol. 28, issue 3, pp. 165–80.

[5] Amitav Acharya, "Will Asia's Past be its Future?". *International Security*, vol. 28, no. 3 (Winter 2003/04), pp. 149–64.

Depicting the spread of Indic ideas and systems to Southeast Asia over a period extending from the fourth to fourteenth century to have been "largely peaceful," the study suggests that there was no clash of civilization between the sources and the recipients of the ideas which were transmitted, and that "the transmission was driven as much by the initiative of local actors as by the cultural entrepreneurship of outsiders." In sum, Amitav concludes that this example of cultural change through time highlights a "powerful historical precedent for inter-civilizational convergence that upholds the agency of local actors and debunks the notion that the diffusion of ideas can only occur through the mechanisms of power politics." At the end of the study, the example of Greek expansion in the Mediterranean — the Hellenization of that region — from the sixth century BCE to the beginning of the Common Era, is presented both as a counter-example to Indianization and as the archetype of later European expansions involving invasion and coercive transformation of other peoples.

* * *

If a thesis is to be accepted, it must be able to withstand critiques. Let us thus take a closer look at this process of diffusion of Indic cultural elements that was allegedly "not accompanied by imperialism, political hegemony or 'colonization' as conventionally understood." That Indic influences permeated Southeast Asia over the period claimed is certainly a truth universally acknowledged.[6] That these influences extended far earlier than the fourth century CE, and perhaps even 800 years before that, is suggested in a recent

---

[6] These are detailed in works such as R.C. Majumdar. *Ancient Indian Colonies in the Far East*, Vol. 1: *Champa*. Lahore, 1927 and Vol. 2: *Suvarnadvipa*. Calcutta, 1937, 1938; G. Coedes. *The Indianized States of Southeast Asia*. (trans. S.B. Cowing) Honolulu: East-West Center Press, 1968.

volume which brings together new scholarship in this field.[7] The mechanisms by which Indic influences — administrative systems, religions, languages and scripts — came to influence Southeast Asia, however, remain elusive. This is partly due to the paucity of sources which we have for this period and, in particular, the dearth of sources relating directly to the modes of interaction between South Asia and Southeast Asia at that time. Ian Mabbett has examined the sources that exist for the "Indianization" of Southeast Asia,[8] and reveals several sources which are suggestive, but somewhat opaque, about the processes by which Indic influences moved into Southeast Asia.

Amitav chooses to dismiss the "occasional mythology about Indian sojourners founding kingdoms in Southeast Asia" (p. 66), preferring to believe that the states established in Southeast Asia were by, for and of "the Southeast Asians." Such dismissal is, of course, congruent with his claims, expressed later in this book that Indic influence in Southeast Asia differed from Greek colonization of the Mediterranean which was "for the Greeks, by the Greeks

---

[7] Pierre-Yves Manguin, A. Mani and Geoff Wade (eds.). *Early Interactions between South and Southeast Asia: Reflections on Cultural Change*. Singapore: Institute of Southeast Asian Studies, 2010.

[8] Ian Mabbett, "The Indianization of Southeast Asia: Reflections on the Historical Sources". *Journal of Southeast Asian Studies*, vol. 8, no. 2 (1977), pp. 143–61. Mabbett highlights two key issues: How did Indian influence spread through Southeast Asia? And how far did Indian influence dominate Southeast Asia? He concludes (p. 145): "The original implantation of Hindu-Buddhist culture may be considered, then, as the initiative of warriors and settlers, traders or local rulers, or some combination of these," and that (p. 161) "In a sense, then, the phrase 'the Indianization of Southeast Asia' enshrines a confusion of categories, for culturally Southeast Asia became nearly as 'Indian' as parts of India, while politically there was no such thing as India." The question, of course, still remains what processes gave rise to this cultural change.

and of the Greeks" (p. 65). The spread of Indian ideas in Southeast Asia also differed, according to this thesis, from Greek colonization by that fact that the latter involved "military conflict" while the former did not. That is to say, unlike the Greeks who established *poleis* for themselves in the process of Hellenization, Indic influence in Southeast Asia was drawn on in an essentially pacific way by Southeast Asians, rather than being imposed.

However, such characterization and dichotomy might be challenged by a closer examination of the sources that we do have for early Southeast Asia. One of the obvious examples of military engagement with Southeast Asia by Indian forces is the attack (or attacks) on Kadaram and other ports on the region by Chola naval ships in the eleventh century.[9] These were, according to an inscription, massive military expeditions across maritime Southeast Asia, and replayed similar military expeditions launched earlier by the Chola rulers against the Rashtrakuta country, Sri Lanka, Bengal and Bihar.[10] However, if perchance, this single inscription by Rājēndra Chola at Thanjavur had been lost to us, we would know nothing of this particular invasion. How then are we to assess that relations in earlier centuries had been pacific, particularly when we read of

---

[9] For which, see Tansen Sen. *Buddhism, Diplomacy, and Trade: The Realignment of Sino-Indian Relations, 600–1400*. Honolulu: University of Hawaii Press, 2003, pp. 221–27; and Tansen Sen. "The Military Campaigns of Rajendra Chola and the Chola-Srivijaya-China Triangle". In *Natapattinam to Suvarnadwipa: Reflections on the Chola Naval Expeditions to Southeast Asia*, edited by Hermann Kulke, K. Kesavapany, and Vijay Sakhuja. Singapore: Institute of Southeast Asian Studies, 2010, pp. 61–75.

[10] For further details, see K.A. Nilakanta Sastri. *The Cōlas*. Madras: University of Madras, 1955, pp. 194–228. It is ironic in the current context that in this volume, Nilakanta Sastri (p. 183) equates Rājēndra with Alexander the Great, one of the great agents of Hellenization.

the "armed guards, swordsmen and mercenaries" who accompanied the traders of Tamil guilds on their travels,[11] and we see suggestive accounts of Funan myths in Classical Chinese texts whereby Funan had been ruled by a *nāgī* princess named Liuye 柳葉, who initially opposed but subsequently submitted and eventually married a seafaring "foreigner" named Huntian 混塡 (Kauṇḍinya?) because she was unable to defend against his magical bow.[12] How are we to understand the allegory of the bow and eventual submission in this account? And how might we construe the Chinese account of Funan in the fourth century, where the ruler Jiao-chen-ru is noted as having originally been an Indian Brahman who received a divine fiat to reign over the polity?[13] Other enigmatic accounts from Sumatra suggest early Tamil military engagement with the island. Edwards McKinnon, in writing on the upland Karo of Sumatra, notes "Among the Sembiring Sinyombak one finds sub-clan or sept names with Dravidian associations such as Colia, i.e., Cōla; Meliala, Malāya, Muham, Pandia etc.; and several others. This is yet another coincidence — during medieval times, it was apparently common for Tamil military units to be named after the titles or epithets of Cōla royalty (Pathmanathan 1976, 122), so possibly the naming of these Karo groups follows a contemporary tradition. The Karo origin stories admit to descent from a mysterious Indian ancestor."[14]

---

[11] For details of whom, see Meera Abraham. *Two Medieval Merchant Guilds of South India*. New Delhi: Manohar, 1988, p. 78.

[12] See Paul Pelliot. "Le Fou-Nan". *Bulletin de l'École française d'Extrême-Orient*, vol. 3 (1903), pp. 248–303, 254; and Michael Vickery, "Funan Reviewed: Deconstructing the Ancients". *Bulletin de l'École française d'Extrême-Orient*, pp. 90–91 (2003), pp. 101–43. See especially p. 102.

[13] Mabbett, I.W. "The Indianization of Southeast Asia," p. 147.

[14] E. Edwards McKinnon. "Continuity and Change in South Indian Involvement in Northern Sumatra: the Inferences of Archaeological

How then should we explain Tamil military unit titles among the
clan names of upland peoples of Sumatra?

The idea of Indic influence on Southeast Asia through time having
been essentially pacific is not new. Neither is the desire to perceive
a softer, more humane form of polity and cultural interaction in
Asia new. The sentiment grew during the period of European high
imperialism, reaching a climax during and following World War
I. Rabindranath Tagore and other pan-Asianists in their quest for
common ideals and common heritage in Asia saw a region whose
components interacted with each other essentially differently from
the West with its "shameless inhumanity."[15]

The scholars associated with the Greater India Society followed with similar ideas. Ramesh Chandra Majumdar was clear
in contrasting the violence of European colonialism to subjugate

Evidence from Kota Cina and Lamreh". In *Early Interactions between South
and Southeast Asia: Reflections on Cultural Change*, edited by Pierre-Yves
Manguin, et al., pp. 137–60. See p. 143.

[15] This ideology is clearly outlined in the opening paragraph of *Ideals of
the East* by Okakura Kakuzō (1862–1913), a prominent pan-Asianist: "Asia
is one. The Himalayas divide, only to accentuate, two mighty civilizations,
the Chinese with its communism of Confucius, and the Indian with its
individualism of the Vedas. But not even the snowy barriers can interrupt
for one moment that broad expanse of love for the Ultimate and Universal,
which is the common thought-inheritance of every Asiatic race, enabling
them to produce all the great religions of the world, and distinguishing
them from those maritime peoples of the Mediterranean and the Baltic,
who love to dwell on the Particular, and to search out the means, not the
end, of life." *The ideals of the East; with special reference to the art of Japan*
(Berkeley: Stone Bridge Classics/Tokyo: IBC Publishing, 2007 reprint). This
is cited in the "Introduction" to Kwa Chong Guan (ed.). *Early Southeast
Asia as Viewed from India; An Anthology from the Journal of the Greater India
Society* (New Delhi: Manohar, forthcoming).

the colonised, vis-à-vis Indian colonization of the Far East, which he considered peaceful, humane, benign and welcomed by the pre-literate natives. Kwa Chong Guan, in his study of the Greater India Society, notes that Majumdar declared in his first major work published by the society:

> [The] ... regeneration of the Cham power in the second century A.D. was due to the introduction of a new element in her politics, viz, the Indian colonists. From this time forward ... [the Chams] ... cheerfully submitted to their foreign masters and adopted their manners, customs, language and religion. They were politically merged in the Indian elements and there was a complete cultural fusion between the two races.[16]

More recently, Sugata Bose of Harvard University and others have pursued this path, stressing the aspirations to Asian universalism by Tagore and others as the feature distinguishing Asian interactions from those which marked the actions and aspirations of western colonial powers.[17] In various ways, although approaching the topic from the domain of international relations theory, Amitav is following in this tradition, with his claims that the modes of Asian expansion — by which Indic ideologies, rituals, religions, statecraft, languages and scripts were imbibed in Southeast Asia — were entirely different from those of the earlier Greek expansions and the later European expansions.[18]

---

[16] From R.C. Majumdar. *Ancient Indian Colonies in the Far East*, Vol 1: *Champa* [f.n. 9] p. 21. Cited in "Introduction" to Kwa (ed.). *Early Southeast Asia as Viewed from India*.

[17] For example, Sugata Bose. *A Hundred Horizons: the Indian Ocean in the Age of Global Empire*. Cambridge, MA: Harvard University Press, 2006.

[18] It should be affirmed, however, that Amitav's thesis assigns Southeast Asians far more agency in Southeast Asian state formation and cultural borrowing than does Majumdar.

However, here is not the place to discuss in detail all the arguments presented in this book. I offer the above thoughts and questions simply to initiate some debate on the issues presented within. The aim of the Nalanda-Sriwijaya Centre Research Series is to make available to the public new and stimulating ideas worthy of debate and it is thus eminently appropriate that this work by Amitav is published in this series. The ideas within these covers will, we hope, induce comment and stimulate argument for years to come.

Geoff Wade
18 October 2012
Singapore

PREFACE

This study revisits one of the most extensive examples of the spread of ideas in the history of civilization: the diffusion of Indian religious and political ideas to Southeast Asia before the advent of Islam and European colonialism. Hindu and Buddhist concepts and symbols of kingship and statecraft helped to legitimize Southeast Asian rulers, and transform the political institutions and authority of Southeast Asia. But the process of this diffusion was not accompanied by imperialism, political hegemony, or "colonization" as conventionally understood. This book investigates different explanations of the spread of Indian ideas offered by scholars, including why and how it occurred and what were its key political and institutional outcomes. My purpose is not to offer an exhaustive account of Indian cultural impact on Southeast Asia, but to draw specific insights from this diffusion to challenge the view that strategic competition is a recurring phenomenon when civilizations encounter each other. It is also to advance the case for considering alternative models of diffusion of ideas and culture in world politics. In essence, I highlight a powerful historical precedent for inter-civilizational convergence that upholds the agency of the local actors and debunks the notion that the diffusion of ideas can only occur through the mechanisms of power politics.

ACKNOWLEDGEMENTS

The original version of this study was written in 2000–01 when I was a Fellow of the Harvard University Asia Center. It was substantially revised and completed during my visiting Professorial Fellowship at the Institute of Southeast Asian Studies (ISEAS) in 2012. I express my deepest gratitude to Ambassador K. Kesavapany, the former director of ISEAS, Dr Tansen Sen, Head of the Nalanda-Sriwijaya Centre at ISEAS and Dr Geoff Wade of the Nalanda-Sriwijaya Centre, for their encouragement and comments. For research in the Mediterranean, I thank the scholars at the Centre for Euro-Mediterranean Studies at the University of Catania, Sicily, and especially Angela Penisi, for their excellent hospitality during my fieldwork in Italy in January-February 2011. I thank two anonymous reviewers for their critical and constructive comments on an earlier draft of this manuscript, and Triena Ong and Mark Iñigo M. Tallara for their excellent editorial input at ISEAS.

Amitav Acharya
February 2012

ABOUT THE AUTHOR

AMITAV ACHARYA is the UNESCO Chair in Transnational Challenges and Governance and Professor of International Relations at the School of International Service, American University, Washington, D.C. He is also the Chair of the American University's ASEAN Studies Center. He is the author of *The Quest for Identity: International Relations of Southeast Asia* (2000); *Constructing a Security Community in Southeast Asia* (2001, 2009); *Whose Ideas Matter: Agency and Power in Asian Regionalism* (2009, 2010), and *The Making of Southeast Asia: International Relations of a Region* (2012). His articles have appeared in *International Organization, International Security, International Studies Quarterly, Journal of Asian Studies, Journal of Peace Research, Pacific Affairs, Pacific Review,* and *World Politics.* He was a Visiting Professorial Fellow at ISEAS and holds the Nelson Mandela Visiting Professorship in International Relations at Rhodes University, South Africa.

1

INTRODUCTION

The cultural influence of one people upon another requires no military occupation, nor the labours of missionaries, not even the peregrinations of hawkers and other traders.

Jan Knappert, *Myths and Folklore in Southeast Asia* (1999: 4)

In considering the imprint of cultural contacts, and the undoubted fact that ideas are imported along with goods, there is a need to develop a more supple language of causal connection than source and imitation, original and copy. The transfer of cultural forms produces a redistribution of imaginative energies, alters in some way a pre-existent field of force. The result is usually not so much an utterly new product as the development or evolution of a familiar matrix.

Stanley J. O'Connor, *The Archaeology of Peninsular Siam* (1986: 7)

Understanding the impact of world views on general politics or foreign policy would require a broader comparative study of cultures.

Judith Goldstein and Robert Keohane, *Ideas and Foreign Policy: Beliefs, Institutions, and Political Chan* (1993: 9)

The interaction among civilizations, including the flow of ideas, culture, and institutions, among them, is increasingly recognized as a powerful force which has shaped world history and still shapes the contemporary international order. (Katzenstein 2010). Since the time Samuel Huntington's "clash of civilizations" thesis appeared (Goldstein and Keohane 1993; Huntington 1993; Huntington 1996), scholars in the social sciences and humanities have debated a number of questions concerning the diffusion of ideas. What is the relationship between ideas and power? Can there be any power in ideas without them being the ideas of the powerful? Do ideas spread peacefully? Where do local actors borrow foreign ideas from and what role do they play in the spread of ideas? And why do some ideas get accepted in a foreign locale while others do not? Do ideas always clash as Huntington suggests? Or do they also converge? What permissive conditions facilitate the convergence of civilizations?

In this study, I urge scholars looking for answers to these questions to turn to a particular narrative in Southeast Asian historiography which can be summarized as follows: (or perhaps earlier) between the fourth and the fourteenth centuries, Indian culture, religions and political ideas played a significant role in the politico-cultural landscape of Southeast Asia (including Funan, Champa, Pagan, Angkor, Srivijaya, Ayutthaya, and Majapahit). These ideas — not just abstract ideas about the divine authority and legitimacy of the ruler, but also specific rules of governance and inter-state relations — influenced the emergence of statehood and the inter-state system in Southeast Asia. Yet the process of their transmission was largely peaceful. There was no clash of civilizations or polities between the sources and the recipients of these ideas. The transmission was driven as much by the initiative of local actors as by the cultural entrepreneurship of outsiders. What was originally viewed to be a passive acceptance by Southeast Asian rulers of foreign, especially Indian ideas, has come to be regarded, thanks to archaeological discoveries and scholarly enquiry and debate, as a matter of proactive and selective borrowing by local rulers seeking to legitimize and empower themselves. In this view, Southeast Asian societies adapted and modified a whole range of foreign ideas and rules to suit the local context. This process preserved and in some cases amplified local beliefs and practices while producing significant but evolutionary historical change in domestic politics and inter-state relations.

This study is inspired by an interest to broaden our understanding of how ideas influence international relations, keeping in mind the statement that "Understanding the impact of world views on general politics or foreign policy would require a broader comparative study of cultures" (Goldstein and Keohane 1993: 9). As a scholar of international relations, I use the insights from Southeast Asian historiography to illustrate how active borrowing and localization is fundamental to normative change in world politics and should receive greater attention from scholars of political science and international relations (Acharya 2009*b*). When civilizations meet, they do not necessarily clash but can cohabit and cooperate. They do not compete, but can learn from each other.

The "classical" period in Southeast Asia constitutes an ideal case for understanding the diffusion of ideas in world civilizations. There is a fair basis to suppose that "ideas made the state" in classical Southeast Asia, just as war, as Charles Tilly famously put it, "made the state" in early modern Europe (Tilly 1975: 42). To analyse how this process of *ideapolitik* unfolded is the primary purpose of this essay.

At this point, let me offer an important clarification about this study. I write as a political scientist, not as a historian. As a political scientist interested in the spread and impact of ideas, my interest is in historiography, rather than history *per se*. Historiography is "a discourse about, but different from, the past" (Munslow 2000: 133). Historiography in this sense has an important place in social constructivist and critical approaches to politics, because these approaches have turned to discourse analysis to offer alternative explanations of international change that challenge rationalist and materialist perspectives. The debate over the Indianization of Southeast Asia constitutes an important example of how discourse can reshape our understanding and explanation of political phenomena, (in this case statehood and regional identity in Southeast Asia). My intended audience in this study is the members of the political science community who have neglected the role of historiography, thereby missing an important opportunity to broaden and enrich their tool-kit for explaining continuity and change in world politics. And I do hope that historians will take kindly and positively to this attempt to draw upon their work and extend it to a different audience, and hopefully the use of political science concepts about power and ideas will also encourage and inform their own thinking and approach to the study of Southeast Asia's past with a broader audience in mind.

2

DEBATING INDIAN INFLUENCE IN SOUTHEAST ASIA

Thanks to its geographic location between two of the largest and oldest civilizations, India and China, and its central place on the classical trade route between China and India extending to the Middle East and Africa, Southeast Asia has been a region with significant exposure to foreign ideas, culture and concepts of statecraft, including Indian, Chinese and Western, throughout history. Not surprisingly therefore, Southeast Asia for a long time was regarded by many as a cultural extension and "lesser version" of India and China, a receptacle of cultural and political ideas from the two. Paul Wheatley draws attention to the importance of Indian influence as a case of transmission of culture and ideas: "the process by which the peoples of western Southeast Asia came to think of themselves as part of Bharatavarsa (even though they had no conception of 'India' as we know it) represents one of the most impressive instances of large-scale acculturation in the history of the world." (Wheatley 1982: 27–28).

Early writings about Southeast Asia reflected a preoccupation with the influence of Indian ideas and culture and to a lesser extent, the influence of other cultures, including Chinese, Islamic and Western. As John Legge put it, "most pre-war studies ... of Southeast Asian history" were marked by "a tendency of scholars to see that history as shaped by influences external to the region rather than as the product of an internal dynamic" (Legge 1992: 6). It was this view which came under attack, especially in the post-World War II period, as a result of new research, archaeological discoveries, and an element of nationalist "imagining" by local scholars about the region's distinctive and "autonomous" past. In the new context, historians asserted Southeast Asia's claim to be a "culturally independent region" (Osborne 1990: 5). Not only did they point to Southeast Asia's distinctive civilizational past pre-dating the advent of Indian and Chinese influences, but also to the resilience of its cultural, social and political features which had survived the coming of foreign influences of all kind. Moreover, the emphasis of the new scholarship was less on how Southeast Asians adopted Indic, or Sinic art, religion, political concepts and practices, and more on how they "adapted these foreign ideas to suit their own needs and values" (Osborne 1990: 5–6). The region's "symbolic and organizational patterns" which were once regarded as being of Indian origin, were now seen to be "merely redefinitions of indigenous institutions" (Wheatley 1982: 27). The argument was that Southeast Asians were not to be "regarded as recipients (or victims) of history, but as makers of it" (Bentley 1985: 299).

In sum, the new scholarship on Southeast Asia moved away from the Indo- and Sino-centric prisms and acknowledged the "right of Southeast Asian countries to be culturally independent units" (Osborne 1979: 13). Initiative and adaptation became the dominant themes; instead of considering the region as a cultural extension of India and China in terms of its "art, religion or political theory", the revisionist view pointed to important variations between Indian and Chinese ideas and practices and those found in Southeast Asia. Among the examples of these variations cited most frequently were: Southeast Asia's rejection of the Indian caste system, the "individual character" of temple art of the Hindu-Buddhist kingdoms of Pagan, Angkor and Java which differed from those of India; and, the nature of Buddha images that were created in Thailand which were "quite different from the images to be found in India" (Osborne 1979: 13). The salience of the nuclear family in Southeast Asia, as opposed to the extended family in India, and the important role of women in traditional peasant society of Southeast Asia represented marked differences between Southeast Asian societies and those of China or India. Historians used a variety of expression to describe the adaptation: how Indian culture and political ideas were "absorbed by the local population and joined to their existing cultural patterns" (Osborne 1979: 24). While Southeast Asian rulers and societies used foreign ideas, they did so selectively. For example, kings used the Indian caste system to describe themselves, but the caste system did not catch on in society at large. Southeast Asian art, while drawing upon Indian models, developed its own distinctive forms. The use of Sanskrit, wide-spread in government and religion, slowly waned as Southeast Asian used Indian scripts to represent their own languages (Osborne 1979: 25). In sum: "Southeast Asians ... borrowed but they also adapted. In some very important cases they did not need to borrow at all" (Osborne 1979: 25). The historiography of Southeast Asia became a project to demonstrate how the region "adopted the alien cultural traits without in the process losing its identity" (Sardesai 1994: 16).

A major target of this revisionist historiography of Southeast Asia was the thesis of "Indianization" of Southeast Asia.[1] Simply and broadly stated, the term "Indianization" may be understood as the extensive diffusion of Indian culture and ideas which had a profound and transformative impact on the culture, society and politics of Southeast Asia.[2] In Southeast Asian historiography, this has been a much debated notion. Manguin cautions that "Indianization has never been a standardized paradigm; definitions have evolved with the passage of time and as the concept became entwined in multiple historicities, each one with its own different cultural background" (Manguin 2011: xiv). But what is important is that the debate over Indianization constituted the basis for a new historiography of Southeast Asia. This in turn offered a number of important concepts that must be counted as major contributions to scholarship on the transmission of ideas and culture in the social sciences and humanities, both classical and modern. These include Jacob van Leur's concept of "local initiative" (van Leur 1955), H.G. Quaritch Wales's notion of "local genius" (Wales 1951); and O.W. Wolters' concept of "localization" and "relocalization" (Wolters 1982 and 1999). It is important to note that while scholars involved in this debate were speaking of the transmission of Indian "cultural ideas," the latter itself was of a broad range, including religion, art,

---

[1] In evaluating the debate over the extent of Indianization of Southeast Asia, it is useful to bear in mind George Coedès' observation that scholars with specialization in Indian culture (Indologists and Sanskritists), usually stressed the deep civilizing role of Indian culture while those trained in social sciences put more emphasis on indigenous initiative and response (Coedès 1968).

[2] Some refer to Indianization as "Hindunization", thereby stressing that the dominant elements in the transmission of Indian ideas were Hindu, not Buddhist, or at least regarding the latter as a subset of the former.

architecture, statecraft, concepts of power, authority and legitimacy, ideas about political stratification, territorial organization, political institutionalization, diplomatic practice, and law. Moreover, these aspects were closely interrelated; as Wolters put it, "art, religion and government are inseparable phenomena in earlier Southeast Asia" (Wolters 1982: 43). But it was not just religious ideas such as divine kingship, which dominated the flow. There were also a number of secular Indian legal, political and diplomatic texts which made their way into the ancient Southeast Asian political landscape. These included the *Manusmriti*, "Code of Manu", the *Dharmashastras* (legal treatises), and above all, the purely secular *Arthasastra*, the most famous Indian classic text on statecraft, all of which were "widely revered" in classical Southeast Asia.[3]

To attempt a detailed examination of this vast and complex historiographical debate is beyond the scope of this study (For aspects of the debate, see Briggs 1948; Bekker 1951; Van Der Kroeff 1951; Du Bois 1951; Bosch 1961; Hall 1960; Smail 1961; Benda 1962; Coedès 1964; Wolters 1981; Wheatley 1982; Legge 1992

---

[3] Cady 1964: 45. The *Arthasastra*, according to D.G.E. Hall, "for centuries was almost the nature of a prescribed textbook at Southeast Asian courts." The text prescribed ideas and norms for both domestic governance and inter-state relations, covering areas such as the pacification of newly-acquired territories; prescriptions regarding maintenance of good customs and abrogation of bad ones; procedures for settling lawsuits; the uses of spies; and the principles for the levying and collection of revenues (Hall 1981: 250). Other Indian influences included the writing systems in Southeast Asia, which with the exception of those of Islamic societies and the Vietnamese, were based on Indian alphabets, as well as the terminologies for law and administration. "Even where the Indian governmental system was not fully introduced, as among the Buginese and the eastern Indonesian islanders, Hindu influences were reflected at the higher levels of social stratification" (Cady 1964: 45).

and Acharya 2000. For an excellent and insightful summary of the debate, see Mabbett 1977*a* and 1977*b*). It will be sufficient to highlight the two closely inter-related questions in this debate, which are especially relevant to our focus on how ideas and norms spread: (1) the process though which Indianization spread through Southeast Asia, and (2) the extent to which it transformed the cultural and political landscapes and institutions of the indigenous states.

The first question itself has two aspects: (1) whether the spread of Indian ideas in Southeast Asia was a matter of "passive acceptance as against active borrowing" (Legge 1992: 8) on the part of Southeast Asians, and (2) the extent to which the borrowed concepts were modified to suit local conditions and needs.

The revisionist historiography found an attractive target in the thesis of Hindu colonization of Southeast Asia, whose most prominent advocate was Indian historian R.C. Majumdar.[4] A particularly blunt expression of his views can be found in the following passage:

> ... intercourse in the region first began by the way of trade, both by land and sea. But soon it developed into regular colonization, and Indians established political authority in various parts of the vast Asiatic continent that lay to the south of China and to the east and southeast of India. Numerous Hindu states rose and

---

[4] The popularity of the colonization thesis has been attributed to nationalism among Indian historians, who were among the keenest advocates of the thesis (although Western — Dutch and French — scholars played their part as well). Some of these scholars were behind the formation of the Greater India Society in Calcutta in 1926. Soon afterwards, Majumdar begun publishing his work on Indian colonization of Southeast Asia. For an excellent overview, see: Basa 1998.

flourished during a period of more than thousand years both on the mainland and in the islands of the Malay Archipelago. Even when the Hindu rule became a thing of the past in India itself, powerful kings bearing Hindu names were ruling over mighty empires in these far-off domains. The Hindu colonists brought with them the whole framework of their culture and civilization and this was transplanted in its entirety among the people who had not yet emerged from their primitive barbarism. (Majumdar 1940: 21)[5]

Majumdar did use the term "colonization" and clearly associated it with the establishment of Hindu political authority. Although there is room to interpret his view to the effect that he was suggesting a possible distinction between rulers who were from India and the "powerful kings bearing Hindu names," meaning that two categories were not the same, because local rulers can adopt Hindu names, generally, one gets the impression of political colonization. Majumdar does not discuss in detail what happened when Indians met with natives, and whether there war or accommodation. The term colonization as used by the Indian historians like Majumdar was not necessarily associated with military conquest (as opposed to having political ramifications). According to Patra, colonization is generally understood to mean "the practice of acquiring colonies by conquest or other means

---

[5] A more cautious and tentative statement of this view could be found in another work by Majumdar, co-authored with two other historians. In this work the authors suggested that "To some such *Khastriya* [Hindu warrior caste] enterprise we perhaps owe the foundation of Indian political power in these far-off regions." But the colonization idea was still prominent: "The Indian colonists established great kingdoms, some of which lasted for more than a thousand years and continued to flourish even long after the end of Hindu rule in India". (Majumdar, Raychaudhuri and Dalta 1948)

and making them dependent. But, the colonizing activity of the ancient Indians was distinctive in several respects. The Indians wherever they went, settled down there, absorbed some of the cultural aspects of the original inhabitants, and adopted some traits of the civilization of the people" (Patra 2010: 17–18). Thus Majumdar's own account of Hindu colonization did not necessarily imply only conquest and control by force, but did suggest large-scale migration.[6] Majumdar himself distinguished Hindu colonization from modern imperialism. Speaking of the Sailendra empire in central Java as a "typical example of the colonial empire of the ancient Hindus", he writes:

> It differs in a striking degree from the conception of a colonial empire in modern times. The Hindus did not regard their colonies as mainly an outlet for their excessive population and an exclusive market for their growing trade. These characteristics of modern colonization were perhaps not altogether absent, but they were not the dominant notes of the colonial policy in ancient India." (Majumdar 1940: 42)

Overall, Majumdar is accused by his critics of giving a hyperbolic picture of Hindu (leaving out Buddhism), domination, or even migration, exaggerating the extent of Hindu exodus as well as the

---

[6] But the extent of Indian migration to Southeast Asia during the ancient times has been controversial. W.F. Wertheim, a Dutch scholar, argues that the "so-called Hindu colonization process, is reduced, in the modern conception, to the presence at the Javanese courts of a comparatively small number of very influential Indian Brahmins, lending political support to Javanese rulers by providing them with a kind of investiture and with a genealogic confirmation of membership in a high caste, and acting at the same time as advisers in affairs of government and things sacral" (Wertheim 1956: 275).

degree of political authority of Hindus from India over Southeast Asia (especially with his use of the term "empire" to describe the political entities that emerged out of Indian migration), and conflating Indian rulers with Indianized Southeast Asian rulers, and Indian colonies with Indianized states under native rulers. His account of Indian "colonization" has also been widely criticised for its overly nationalistic tone and cultural arrogance. But despite his unabashed assertion of the superiority of the Hindu culture, Majumdar concedes that even this superior culture had to adapt to some extent to the beliefs and habits of the native population and undergo modification, if not at source (back in India), but at the point of diffusion or at the recipient's end:

> Wherever they settled they [Indians in Southeast Asia] introduced, to the fullest extent, the elements of culture and civilization of the motherland. Their religious and social institutions, and their language, art and letters, almost completely superseded those of the people among whom they lived. They themselves became children of the soil and made the colonies their only home. They never kept aloof from the native population and merged themselves into the indigenous society. They ... intermarried with them and formed a new but homogenous population and society. By virtue of its inherent superiority, the Hindu culture no doubt formed the dominant element in this fusion, but it was also influenced considerably by the impact of new ideas. The Hindu social institutions were adapted to the needs and habits of the people, and both religion and literature were transformed to a certain extent by the influence of the indigenous elements. (Majumdar 1940: 42)

Elsewhere also, he and fellow historians made some concession to the indigenous adaptation of Hindu culture. "Hindu customs and manners were no doubt modified to some extent by coming into contact with these peoples" and there was "a gradual fusion between the two races", but "still for a thousand years the essential features of Indian civilization were the dominant characteristics of society in these regions" (Majumdar, Raychaudhuri and Datta 1948: 215–6). Hence, to some extent, Majumdar shows an awareness that the diffusion of Indian ideas and culture was not a one-way street, focusing only on what Indians gave to Southeast Asians, not what they might have learnt from native cultures. (I should stress again, however, that his account of Indians learning from Southeast Asians applies only to migrant Hindus who remained permanently in Southeast Asia. He does not talk about whether Southeast Asian culture travelled back to India). Nonetheless there was a hint in his account that the Indian cultural interactions with Southeast Asians might have been a two-way street of mutual influence. Moreover, his account need not be incompatible, at least in one respect, with the alternative local initiative thesis, to be discussed below, which holds that Indians were called upon by Southeast Asian rulers to satisfy their own political aspirations. The two processes, migration by Indians in search of trade and privilege, and the calling upon of Indian culture by Southeast Asians for their own needs of political legitimation could go hand-in-hand.

If Majumdar represents one extreme of the "Indianization" debate, at the other extreme stands J.C. van Leur, a Dutch economic historian and colonial official in Indonesia (van Leur 1955). He was particularly dismissive of the colonization thesis. His views can be examined in relation to two different modes of thinking about the spread of Indian culture to Southeast Asia. The first, known as the *khastriya* (warrior) theory, saw the transmission of Indian ideas as the result of direct Indian conquest and colonization of large parts of Southeast Asia. The second, the so-called *vaisya* (merchant) theory — emphasized the role of Indian traders with their extensive commercial interactions with Southeast Asia, who brought with them not just goods, but also Indian cultural artefacts and political ideas (Mabbett 1977*b*: 143–44). But these theories were rejected by van Leur (in a thesis written in 1934, but published in 1955 after his untimely death). Van Leur found no evidence that the Indian approach to Southeast Asia amounted to conquest; on the contrary, he considered it to have been through peaceful means. He also refuted that the transmission of Indian ideas had been the handiwork of Indian traders despite substantial commercial linkages between India and Southeast Asia. The Indian trading class, being mostly peddlers (Southeast Asian trade was mostly of the pre-capitalist, peddling type), could not be expected to have mastered the complexities of Hindu ideas and political organization to appear credible before their Southeast Asian recipients. Since Indian influence was most directly evident in Southeast Asian royal courts, and involved matters of high culture such as "art, literature, ideas of power, sovereignty and kingship" (Legge 1992: 8), it must have been the work of the *brahmins* (the Indian priests) who alone possessed the mastery of "sacral magical power and sacral religion" (van Leur 1955: 357). The *brahmins* were actively solicited by Southeast Asian rulers who wanted to learn from Indian ideas about political organization that, thanks to their relatively organized form and their heavy emphasis on magic and mystery, offered an attractive way of enhancing the ruler's legitimacy and authority. In this respect, Indian ideational influence in Southeast Asia was largely a matter of "deliberate Southeast Asian borrowing of ideas, artistic styles and modes of political organization" which helped the emergence, consolidation and enlargement of local polities (Legge 1992: 8). To cite van Leur:

> The initiative for the coming of Indian civilization [to Southeast Asia] emanated from the Indonesian ruling groups, or was at least an affair of both the Indonesian dynasties and the Indian hierocracy. That cultural influence had nothing to do with trade. The course of events amounted essentially to a summoning to Indonesia of

Brahman priests, and perhaps alongside them of Indian *condottieri*
and Indian court artificers … Indian priesthood was called eastwards
— certainly because of its wide renown — for the magical, sacral
legitimation of dynastic interests and the domestication of subjects,
and probably for the organization of the ruler's territory into a state.
(van Leur 1955: 103–4)

In describing the process of Indianization through local initiative, van Leur borrowed heavily from Max Weber's explanation of
the spread of Hinduism from a small region of North India to
the entire Indian subcontinent[7] (Kulke 1993: 240–161; Wertheim
1954). A key thesis of Weber was "external Hinduization." This
described how the rulers of pre-Aryan tribes of central and south
India came under Hindu influence by "calling upon" *Brahmanas*
from the north. The process was marked by voluntary initiative,
rather than coercion and conquest and it was driven by the desire
among the local elite for legitimation. The common point of the
arguments of Weber and van Leur was that "neither the pre-Aryan
tribes of central and South India nor those in Southeast Asia were
subdued by invaders who superimposed their statecraft and culture

---

[7] The form of social interaction and ideational adaptation described by
van Leur is by no means unique. He compares the spread of Hindu ideas
in Southeast Asia to the "way German civilization of the Middle Ages
extended its influence far beyond the limits of German group colonization,
in the same way the Graeco-Byzantine hierocracy set its stamp on the
civilization of Russia." (van Leur 1955: 104). This again was an analogy he
had borrowed from Weber, who himself had used it to describe the spread
of Hinduism from northern India to the south: "As the Slavic princes of
the East called into their lands German priests, knights, merchants, and
peasants, so the kings of the East Ganges Plain and of Southern India, up
to the Tamils at the southern trip, called upon Brahmans trained in writing
and administration". (Weber 1958: 16 f)

upon them...". Instead, "Both in India (according to Weber) and Indonesia (according to van Leur) it was the indigenous rulers who invited or 'summoned' (van Leur) the *Brahmanas* to their courts, primarily for the purpose of legitimation of their new social status." Weber's theory of legitimation was key to van Leur's perspective that refuted the dominant *Khastriya* theory of Indianization of Southeast Asia. "The struggle for or against acceptance of Hinduism" Weber had argued, "generally was led by the rulers or ruling strata; in any case the strongest motive for the assimilation of Hinduism was undoubtedly the desire for legitimation" (Weber 1920: 18). According to Weber, the motive for accepting Hindunization lay in the fact that it "not only endowed the ruling stratum ... with a recognized rank in the cultural world of Hinduism, but, through their transformation of castes, secured their superiority over the subject classes with an efficiency unsurpassed by any other religion" (Weber 1958: 16). Van Leur similarly argued that the rulers of Southeast Asia in an "attempt at legitimizing their interest ... and organizing and domesticating their states and subjects ... called Indian civilization to the east — that is to say, they summoned the Brahman priesthood to their courts" (van Leur p. 98).

Certain aspects of the *process* of ideational transmission implicit in van Leur's analysis (what has been called "the Idea of the Local Initiative" and which may also be called as the *Brahmana* thesis) deserve emphasizing here. The act of "borrowing" was mostly the work of the ruling elite. The general population was relatively unaffected by Hindu ideas. (This was the case due to the fact the hierarchy of the Indian caste system would have prevented interaction between Brahmins and lower strata of population). More importantly, the borrowing of Indian culture and political concepts was done in a highly selective manner. Quite clearly, the Indonesian rulers found attractive those Indian ideas that helped to legitimize their rule. Van Leur urges the consideration of "the Indonesian ruler on Java as a person who had royal investiture conferred on him" by Hindu concepts of power and authority. Hindu ideas and priests helped to legitimize Indonesian rulers by having "a mythological Indian genealogy assigned to him" (van Leur 1995: 109).

3

"INDIANIZATION", "LOCALIZATION" OR "CONVERGENCE"?

If Majumdar and van Leur represent the two ends of the debate over "Indianization," a newer perspective accords significant local autonomy and agency to Southeast Asians without dismissing the impact of Indian ideas. It accepts the view that Indian ideas did inspire political change and development in Southeast Asia, but this was neither a case of "wholesale transplantation" nor did it acquire the character of a "thin, flaking glaze" (van Leur 1995: 95).

O.W. Wolters, in a major reinterpretation of Southeast Asian regional political history, provides further evidence and argumentation to illuminate the political motivations behind the Southeast Asian rulers' borrowing of Indian ideas. Wolters argues that the transmission of Indian ideas is best described as a process of "local construction" by Southeast Asian rulers in search of greater authority and legitimacy. Wolters believed that pre-Indic kingship in Southeast Asia was "cognatic" in nature, marked by a relative indifference towards lineage descent (as well as recognition of descent through either male or female offspring). In this situation, there existed numerous small territorial units which could only be occasionally centralized through the personal efforts of a "man of prowess" — a "big man" who was thought to possess a lot of "soul stuff" (a concentration of spiritual power) (Wolters 1982: 4–5). But the rule by such "men of prowess" was limited in scope and would not usually survive his death. In this context, the arrival of Hindu devotional ideas filled an important gap in a ruler's search for authority and legitimacy. A Southeast Asian ruler could now identify himself with Indian divine figures to augment his innate "soul stuff" and develop a more enduring basis of power. As Wolters puts it, such "construction of Hindu devotionalism ... led to heightened self-perceptions among the chieftain class and prepared the ground for overlords' claims to universal sovereignty, based on Siva's divine authority" (Wolters 1982: 52). Wolters provides evidence of this process in Cambodia, whose kings developed the *Devaraja* (god-king) cult beginning with Jayavarman II's inauguration in AD 802. The *Devaraja* cult "assimilated the king's spiritual identity to Siva as 'the king of gods,' a definition of Siva that matched the overlord status that the king had already achieved" (Wolters 1982: 7).

The general thrust of van Leur's thesis has been accepted by many historians when they consider how external influences on Southeast Asia came about and the extent to which they led to the transformation of the cultural and political landscape of Southeast Asia.[1] Yet, despite being a turning point in Southeast Asian histori-

---

[1] Hermann Kulke writes: "... nowadays no research on Southeast Asian history is thinkable on the basis of the status quo ante — before the translation of van Leur's thesis was published in the year 1955. Van Leur's emphasis on the 'primacy of indigenous (Southeast Asian) initiative' has thus to be regarded as a major contribution to modern Southeast Asian studies" (Kulke 1993: 261).

ography, it has not remained challenged. In the best available review of the literature on Indianization, Mabbett argues that van Leur's "extremism [in dismissing the scope and extent of Indian cultural influence in Southeast Asia] has not been emulated ... more recent writers have stressed the interaction between the local and import-ed cultures" (Mabbett 1977*b*: 144). This "extremism" he refers to concerns van Leur's outright rejection of all foreign influence, or his view that the influence of all foreign religions and cultural forms on Indonesia was but "a thin and flaking glaze" (van Leur 1955: 95).[2] But few would question van Leur's rejection of the *khastriya* thesis, or the view that Indian influence in Southeast Asia was the result of outright conquest. On this count, the most important known examples of Indian military campaigns in Southeast Asia were two attacks carried out by the Chola king Rajendra Chola, in 1025 and 1047 respectively, allegedly to retaliate against Srivijayan interference in Chola trade with China (Sen 1999: 61). This was far from a common or recurring pattern so far as Indian contacts with Southeast Asia were concerned. The "Local Initiative" thesis associated with van Leur has also been supported by those, such as F.D.K. Bosch who pointed to the lack of references to Indian conquests in Southeast Asian inscriptions (Bosch 1961). Bosch also argued that Indian influence was stronger in inland kingdoms than coastal regions, suggesting a minimal role of traders as transmitter of ideas (Bosch 1961). Coedès believes that an initial process of transmission of Indian ideas by traders could have laid the foundation for Southeast Asian polities and prepared them to receive, on their own initiative, Indian concepts of kingship and power (Coedès 1968). However, "the initiative for the Indianizing process in Southeast Asia most certainly

---

[2] "The sheen of world religions and foreign cultural forms is a thin and flaking glaze; underneath it the whole of the old indigenous forms has continued to exist" (van Leur 1955: 95).

came from the region's ruling classes who invited Brahmans to serve at their courts as priests, astrologers and advisers" (Sardesai 1994: 17). Paul Wheatley argues that while local Southeast Asian rulers used Indian ideas to enhance their status, this was a dynamic social process in which both local and Indian ideas and culture played a vital role (Wheatley 1964, and 1973). Some scholars argue that there was "an approximately equality between giving and receiving cultures" (Mabbett 1977: 144; see also: Groslier 1960: 10). J.G. de Casparis urged historians to adopt a more complex picture than the "relatively simple, or perhaps simplistic, view of Indianization." While it was not his "intention to demolish existing theories about 'Indianization',," he wished to "call attention to some of their weakness and so to [sic] prepare the way for a more satisfactory approach." To that end, he conceptualized the cultural flow between India and Indonesia as a two-way street, marked by a "complicated network of relations, both between various parts of each of the two great regions and between the two regions themselves," and having elements that might have led to Indonesian influence in India, rather than just vice-versa (de Casparis 1983: 4,7, cited in Kulke 2006: 13–14).

As hinted at earlier, Southeast Asians were not undiscriminating in their borrowing of Indian ideas and practices. Only those which conformed to pre-existing indigenous patterns (as well as the economic and political needs of the local elite, including their desire for power and legitimacy, which we have already seen in the case of van Leur's thesis concerning local initiative) were more likely to have been acquired or accepted when they were presented before Southeast Asians. Cady argues that the "local genius" shaped the preferences for which foreign ideas would be "congenial" to the local matrix. Thus, he associates the preference for Siva over Visnu in eastern Java, Cambodia and Champa with the pre-existing practice of "fertility and ancestral rites, combined with deification of the life-giving power of the soil". The Siva linga, which represented the essence of royalty, could similarly be seen in the context of the pre-existing local practice of planting an "upright stone symbolizing the fertility god of the earth" (Cady 1964: 45).

Some Indian cultural institutions and practices were summarily rejected or significantly modified so that they scarcely resembled the original Indian idea. Among the foremost examples of this is the Indian caste system (*varna*), which found little acceptance in Southeast Asia, despite superficial similarities. Mabbett points out that *varna* in Angkor was institutionalized and practiced differently than in India (Mabbett 1977*c*). In India, caste was a general division of the population, while in Angkor it applied to divisions of elite groups at the royal court. Brahmin status was less important and exalted in Angkor (Wheatley 1982: 27). The Burmese rejected aspects of Manu's law concerning marriage. Hooykaas has identified several features of Balinese Hinduism which are different from the Indian version. These include the Balinese belief that one is reborn within one's groups of relatives, that gods normally live in mountains and lakes and not in temples, and that cremation should be performed only depending on one's social position (Hooykaas p. 25, cited in Wolters 1982: 59). Another, rather unsavoury aspect of Indian culture that some historians believe to have been rejected by Southeast Asians was the subordination of women. Overall then, there is little evidence of wholesale adoption of Indian ideas. Instead, the evidence points to selective learning on the basis of local preferences and agency. As Cady puts it, "Southeast Asian peoples appear to have oscillated between their appropriation of Indian forms and the resurgence of pre-Indian standards of civilization" (Cady 1964: 45).

Furthermore, those ideas which had appeal and those which had some but not total appeal were modified to suit local need and to project indigenous or pre-existing beliefs, practices and institutions. This leads to another major aspect of the process whereby Indian ideas were transmitted to classical Southeast Asia, and it is this aspect which lies at the heart of the process of what Wolters termed as "localization".

Wolters conceives of localization as a "local statement ... into which foreign elements have retreated."[3] In introducing the concept in the context of Indianization, Wolters writes that through localization:

> Indian materials tended to be fractured and restated and therefore drained of their original significance ... The materials, be they words, books, or artifacts, had to be localized in different ways before they could fit into various local complexes of religious, social, and political systems and belong to new cultural "wholes." Only when this had happened would the fragments make sense in their new ambience, the same ambience which allowed the rulers and their subjects to believe that their centers were unique (Wolters 1999: 55).[4]

The concept of localization (and its corollary- "re-localization") explains how different parts of Southeast Asia reflected different degrees of congruence with Indian ideas, language, religions, art, architecture and law. Thus, to study how foreign ideas impacted Southeast Asia was to study "processes behind the endless elaboration of new local-foreign cultural 'wholes'" in which local actors and

---

[3] Wolters, 1999: 57. In analyzing Wolters' localization concept, I have used the first edition of his book. A new and expanded edition was published in 1999.

[4] Wolters' concept of localization is similar to "adaptation", or "synthesis" or "syncretism". But he prefers "localization" because the other terms "seem to shirk the crucial question of where and how foreign elements began to fit into a local culture. 'Adaptation' and 'synthesis' give an impression of the outcome of the process, while 'syncretism' does likewise and also begs the question by conveying a dictionary sense of reconciliation of originally contradictory differences. The three terms smother the initiative of the local elements responsible for the process and the end product." (Wolters 1982: 53).

norms acted as a prism through which foreign ideas were adapted. As Wolters put it, "local beliefs, operating under cultural constraint, were always responsible for the initial form the new 'wholes' took" (Wolters 1982: 53).

For example, differences in the practice of Theravada Buddhism between Thailand and Burma are a case of localization: a greater emphasis was placed on metaphysics in Burma than in Thailand, while monastic discipline was more emphasized in Thailand than in Burma. Buddhists in Burma placed more emphasis on the institution of the noviciate, while Thais emphasized monkhood (Wolters 1982: 48). Similarly, varying uses of Sanskrit in the region offers an example of re-localization; in Champa, for example, Sanskrit continued till fifteenth century, while in Cambodia it remained dominant till the fourteenth century and in Java, only until the tenth century (Wolters 1982: 47). "Not only did Indian materials have to be localized everywhere but those which had been originally localized in one part of the region would have to be relocalized before they could belong elsewhere in the same sub-region" (Wolters 1982: 53–54). Thus, cultural adaptation is not just about how non-Southeast Asian ideas were adjusted and altered leading to variations between India and Southeast Asia, but also about how different parts of Southeast Asia developed variations of the same outside influence.

To further illustrate his localization thesis, Wolters shows how the Burmese adjusted the Indian legal text of Manu when it was introduced in Burma, rejecting the latter's notion of marriage, while in Champa and Cambodia, "local practice" was reflected in similar deviations from Indian legal texts were made with respect to property and land (Hooker 1978: 35–36). Another example of localization is how Indian law texts were adapted in Indonesia. M.B. Hooker provides an important example of how Indian ideas "decorated" Southeast Asian substance. One of the Indian legal practices adopted by the Javanese was that of *Jayapatra,* or "note of victory". It was a document stating the fact that a case had been settled. It contained a statement by both parties to the litigation, the evidence considered, and the particular text of law, or *smrti*, applied, and the judgement itself, with the seal (The earliest *Jayapatras* in Java date from AD 907). But some of the *Jayapatras* found in Java do not make reference to Indian law texts. Moreover, while in India the trial was usually conducted by a judge (*pradivaka*), in Java, it was conducted by a judge-arbitrator (*samget*), who was "assisted by a council of notables whose decisions were of a collegiate nature." The proceedings of the trial in Java "seem to have been in the nature of searching for a compromise, thus negating the need for the citation of *smrti*, a reference to which need not necessarily be basic to a decision." Thus, the Javanese practice appears to have been an important localization of the Indian system,[5] in which the *Jayapatra* served as a "form for recording a decision based upon an Indian model but did not require the application of principles of Indian law" (Hooker 1978: 35–36).

Other scholars developed similar concepts, stressing adaptation and localization, rather than transplantation and wholesale adoption. One of the main examples, can be found in religion. Buddhism came from India, but "developed unique ways in Southeast Asia" (Keyes 1992: 18). This may be why Buddhism flourished in Southeast Asia while in India, the religion withered. Islam originated in the Middle East, but the Southeast Asian version of Islam is much more moderate than in the Middle East. Localization applied not

---

[5] There are important parallels between the localization of *Jayapatra* and the modern notion of consultations and consensus, an ASEAN Way which is usually traced to Javanese village culture. The consensus process is also characterized by a rejection of strict textual legalism and formal arbitration and involves a search for compromise through consultations.

just to Indian ideas, but also Chinese ones, especially in Vietnam. In Vietnam, which had been under Chinese control for 1,000 years, a new legal code issued in 1042, though modelled on the Tang code, reflected "the adjustments that would have been made elsewhere in the region to accommodate local social norms" (Wolters 1982: 46–7). The aim was to have a social code "organized and presented so that classes of subject matter would constitute a body of law that was clear and appropriate to the times" (Wolters 1982: 47). In literature too, one can find examples of indigenous resilience. Vietnamese literature is not to be regarded as a "provincial branch" of Chinese literature, since much of it was not written in Chinese characters, and that which was "was often unique to Vietnam in both style and substance" (Keys 1992: 18). Osborne argues from an examination of Vietnamese cultural and political traditions that the "strength of non-Chinese cultural life," especially outside the court "belies any picture of that country as a mere receiver of ideas, unable to offer traditions of its own" (Osborne 1979: 13–14).

Other examples of localization of Indian ideas by Southeast Asian rulers so as to make them conform to local tradition can be found in the Balinese conceptions of the Hindu gods, Siva and Visnu. In Indian mythology, Visnu is the Protector who reincarnates periodically to save the world from calamity. In Bali, Visnu is localized to become a "rising prince," who emerges from the periphery to infuse the community with new spiritual energy and status. This localization of Visnu can be understood in the context of "the Balinese cultural background", which "is one in which new men appear from time to time from the fringes of extensive and ascendant ancestor-groups, build up networks of alliances by demonstrating their capacity for leadership, and eventually become ancestors in a particular generation by virtue of their achievements during their lifetime on behalf of their kindred. Localization in

Bali means that Visnu's periodic reappearances fit into a Balinese statement constrained by local mechanisms for social mobilization" (Wolters 1982: 59).

As mentioned before, such dynamics of adaptation and localization of religious ideas was by no means confined to the spread of Hindu and Buddhist ideas from India, but could be found in later ages of Southeast Asian history. Anderson offers one major example in analysing the spread of Islam in Java:

> The penetration of Islam was more assimilative than revolutionary ... after an initial period of zealotry, the devout Islamic groups were more or less absorbed into the patrimonial state ... after the fifteenth century, the rulers assumed Islamic titles, kept Islamic officials in their entourage, and added Islam to the panoply of their attributes. Yet this overt Islamization of the rulers does not seem to have caused major alterations in their way of life or outlook. The penetration of Islam scarcely changed the composition and the recruitment of the Javanese political elite or affected the basic intellectual framework of traditional political thought. To use Gramsci's term, at no point did a "hegemonic" Islamic culture develop in Java (Anderson 1990: 68).

Anderson's invoking of Gramsci is interesting, as it shows that outside ideas, no matter how powerful, do not supplant the fundamental beliefs and ways of life. Rather, they are adapted and localized. This is not to say that these outside ideas do not have any impact. Anderson provides an important example of how outside ideas can induce change in local beliefs. Sometimes, outside ideas can have a "rationalizing" impact on traditional beliefs. Anderson shows how Western ideas associated with the advent of Dutch capitalism and technology and rational secularism in the late nineteenth century generated reform movements in traditional Javanese Islam. In Java, "almost every component of traditional Islam, except fundamental articles of faith, was subjected to this rationalizing tendency" (Anderson 1990: 68). These reform movements came into conflict with traditional Islamic elements. This ideational contestation was played out within Javanese society between reformist and traditional groups. This suggests how external ideas can be adapted by sections of local society. In other words, localization can lead to normative change, altering traditional beliefs.

The impact of localization, or the adaptation of foreign ideas and beliefs to suit local context and needs, also comes through clearly and powerfully in studies of Southeast Asian art history, with distinct parallels to the region's government and politics. H.G. Quaritch Wales in his study of Southeast Asian art history sought to "demonstrate the part played by local genius in actually guiding the evolution of the Indianized civilization itself" (Wales 1951: 83). Looking at intra-regional differences in art between Java, Champa, and Cambodia (see the images of Borobudur, Angkor and Champa in the photo section), he concluded that these differences could be explained by local genius, since the Indian influence was common to all. Wales studied the differences between Cham and Khmer temples and noted that while the former preferred tall sanctuary towers, the latter chose to build their temples in the form of stepped pyramids (compare the images of the Bayan, Cambodia, and the Cham towers at Po Nagar, Po Klung Garai and Po Rome in the photo section). While both were influenced by Indian religion, the differences reflected preexisting local beliefs and practices: the Khmers worshipped the earth, while the Chams worshipped the sky (Wolters 1982: 47). Wales concluded, "The Indian share was more active in terms of stimulus, but the local contribution certainly showed no less activity in terms of response" (Wales 1951: 195). Wales' study also concluded that when a foreign influence decays, there is a return to indigenous forms and practice. Thus, the art of Majapahit (a Javanese kingdom), may be seen as a degeneration of an Indian form, but "Majapahit art is not the product of a degeneration, but springs from virile resurgence" (Wales 1951:198). "Local genius gives direction to evolution" (Wales 1951: 198).

Examples of local genius can also be found in language, how Sanskrit loan words were used. Many Sanskrit words of religious and cultural meanings were adapted and expressed in a peculiarly Javanese manner (Gonda 1952: 202). Ferdinand de Saussure's work on loan words show how "a loan word no longer counts as such whenever it is studied within a [linguistic] system; it exists only through its relation with, and opposition to, words associated with it ..." (de Saussure 1966: 22). Wolters uses the case of some Sanskrit words to illustrate localization and local genius. This shows variations not only with India, but also between parts of Southeast Asia. *Santosa* in Sanskrit means "contemplation" or "satisfaction", but it was naturalized by the Javanese "to signify what was important to them," which is "the ideal state of mind of the 'completely unconcerned' man in control of all passions." The adaptation reflected a "Javanese social collectivity" (Wolters 1982: 50). The usage of *sakti*, the Sanskrit term for "power" is of special interest: In Javanese, *sakti* means "the creating power of divinities", while in Toba Batak (Sumatra), *sokti* denotes ability to make a successful prediction, or when "pronouncements or predictions are borne out by the facts or verified", while in Bali, *sakti* means "ancestral power" (Wolters 1982: 50).

The evidence of local genius and local reconstruction in Southeast Asian art history could be extended to other areas. As Wheatley put it: "It has often been pointed out that, although the great architectural monuments such as the Bayon and the Borobudur — and there is no reason to exclude innumerable minor structures as well — are without analogues in India itself, yet their meaning is intelligible only to the student of Indian culture. What is less often remarked is that in ancient times the same principle held for institutions of government, administration, exchange, and symbolism — or so I believe" (Wheatley 1982: 27).

While art and architecture, along with inscriptions, were central to the earlier understanding of and debate over Indianization, including the rejection of the "Indian colonization" thesis, a newer set of insights that confirms the localization perspective comes from archaeology. One reason for the "Indian colonization" thesis in particular had to do with the sources used to study Southeast Asia's past. These came mostly from epigraphy and the history of art and architecture, favoured by Indologists. In these earlier debates, inputs from archaeological studies were limited to findings from religious monumental remains. Since Sanskrit inscriptions and stone or brick temples with Indian deities emerged only after the first centuries of the Common Era, this created the impression that Southeast Asians lacked an indigenous civilization until the arrival of Indian religion and political ideas. However, recent archaeological findings confirm the existence of extensive early trade links between India and Southeast Asia, especially trade in artefacts. This has given rise to the view not only that Southeast Asia had come into contact with India for several centuries — a "millennium-long phase of exchange" (Manguin 2011: xvi) before the hitherto accepted beginning of Indianization, between the third and fifth centuries CE, but also that in this process, Southeast Asians may have had even greater agency than the critics of the conventional Indianization thesis (or the proponents of "autonomous history") had assumed. To quote Manguin, the findings of new archaeological research makes it:

> necessary to conclude that by the time Indian-inspired temples, statues and epigraphy appeared in Southeast Asia, sometime between the third and the fifth century CE, the relationship between Southeast Asian and Indian societies had already come a very long way. We are now far removed from the tenets of the Greater India Society and the imagined vision of a sudden imposition of Indian culture, as a *deus ex machina*. In other words, one is entitled to raise the question as to whether Southeast Asia was Indianized before 'Indianization' (Manguin 2011: xix–xx).

In other words, archaeological research not only confirms the agency of the local in Southeast Asia; it also makes for even greater Southeast Asian agency, by adding artisans to the list of other better known agents, such as traders, priests and warriors (Manguin 2011: xix).

I now turn to another question posed at the previous chapter (page 10): what was the outcome of the process of localization? What sort of change came out of it? It may seem that localization is a form of resistance to change and preference for status quo. But this is not the case; Southeast Asian societies did change when they localized foreign ideas and materials. Thus, localization does not mean the Southeast Asian societies remain unchanged. Localization is not resistance to change, but is selective change that conforms to local needs. It's a process that brings about greater synergy between the outside or foreign and the inside or the local. In such a process, indigenous beliefs do not disappear, but they are made more systematic, accessible, and even amplified. The result is progress, but it is progress consistent with local aspirations and needs.

As I have mentioned earlier, ideas transmitted from India might have helped Southeast Asia's small chiefdoms under "men of prowess" to become more legitimate and durable kingdoms. As a further elaboration, one of the earliest examples of such cultural and political transformation brought about by Indian ideas can be seen in inscriptions found at Kutei on the River Mahakam, a rich source of gold in Kalimantan. These inscriptions mention a local ruler Mulavarman (Sanskrit), who was the son of Asvavarman (Sanskrit) and grandson of Kundunga (non Sanskrit). These inscriptions show him as:

> An established king (*rajan, rajendra, nrap, narendra*) as defined by the
> Indian model, within the classic Indian caste system (*–varman* being
> a *Khastriya*, or *warrior caste*, name ending), yet stemming from the

country he ruled, as grandson of the local chief (Kundunga). The king, Mulavarman, was surrounded by priests (*vipra, dvijendra*), who made, erected, and inscribed stone stelae which they called sacrificial posts (*yupa*)" (Maxwell 2007: 76).

The inscriptions record ritual sacrifices by the king and gifts he gave to the priests for conducting the rites. This shows that a local person (perhaps the descendant of what Wolters would call "a man of prowess") was using Indian concepts, structures and symbols, to establish his legitimacy and authority and transform himself from a chief to a king.[6] What is also clear that the ruler is not an Indian, but as his grandfather's name indicate, a native of the area, who adopted a Sanskrit name. Maxwell contends that while the authenticity of some of the claims pertaining to the rulers wealth and power recorded in these inscriptions may be doubted, the ruler "was using formulaic expressions borrowed from Indian sources as part of his apparatus he was employing to define his role" (Maxwell 2007: 76).

The legitimation of kingship occurred mainly through the idea of divine kingship. Those rulers who accepted Hinduism identified with Siva (as in Champa, and in fourteenth century Majapahit) or Visnu (as in the case of King Airlangga in eleventh century Java, and Suryavarman II in twelfth century Cambodia) (Heine-Geldern 1956: 8–9). In Cambodia and Champa, the cult of a lingam often symbolized the "essence of divine kingship" (Heine-Geldern 1956: 9). Moreover, the location of temples at the centre of the kingdom was important. "As the universe, according to Brahman and Buddhist ideas, centers around Mount Meru, so that smaller universe, the

---

[6] This view has been challenged by de Casparis who proposed that the Kutei inscriptions of Eastern Kalimantan of about AD 400 may well refer to an Indonesian rather than Indian ceremonial practice (de Casparis 1983: 7, cited in Kulke 2006: 13–14).

empire was bound to have a Mount Meru in the center of the capital which would be if not in the country's geographical, at least in its magic center" (Heine-Geldern 1956: 4).

Not only did this borrowing of Indian ideas helped establish the ruler's political authority and legitimacy, it also facilitated economic and commercial activities related to the gold reserves of the area. As Maxwell puts it in the context of the Kutei inscriptions of Mulavarman, "Without these Indian structures — the definition of a king with his entourage of specialized priests and at least the rudiments of legitimizing Vedic religion with its ritual paraphernalia — the kind of social organisation required for any monopoly on and exploitation of the gold resources of the Mahakam, plus the international connections needed to trade in them from a small harbor on the east coast of Kalimantan, would most probably not have been possible" (Maxwell 2007: 76, 79). Maxwell proposes that a similar dynamic of cultural and political transformation of Southeast Asia brought about by Indian ideas might have occurred in other parts of Southeast Asia, including Champa and West Java during the earliest phases of Indian influence.

Sheldon Pollock's notion of "Sanskrit cosmopolis" offers a novel conceptualization of the institutional outcome of the diffusion of Indian culture and political ideas into Southeast Asia. The Sanskrit cosmopolis describes "largely hierarchized societies, administered by a corps of functionaries, scribes, tax collectors, living in grand agrarian cities geometrically planned in orientation to the cardinal points and set within imaginary geographies that ... recapitulated the geography of India" (Pollock 1996: 14–15). The idea of the Sanskrit cosmopolis offers two important insights that are relevant to the central argument of this study. The first is the claim about the peaceful nature of the process through which it reproduced itself. The Sanskrit cosmopolis was not the result of any Indian military conquest or geopolitical expansion. As Pollock writes, "Constituted by no imperial power or church but in large part by a communicative system," the Sanskrit cosmopolis was "characterized by a trans-regionally shared set of assumptions about the basics of power" (Pollock 1996: 14). Second, by its very nature, the Sanskrit cosmopolis lent itself to 'adoption and localization' rather than outright replication. Comparing the cosmopolis with the Romanization in the Mediterranean region, Pollock argues that the Sanskrit language itself permitted greater "vernacularization" than Latin did in the context of Romanization (Pollock 2006: 270).[7] Moreover:

> Whatever the status of *dharma* in the Sanskrit cosmopolitan conceptual order, practical law remained resolutely local ... The supposedly built-in afflictions of Sanskrit culture — caste, patriarchy, Brahmanical power, and the like — are hard to demonstrate as necessary concomitants to the cosmopolitan package ... Nor do we find in the Sanskrit cosmopolis anything comparable to the influence exerted by a core culture in a center-periphery world-system relationship that we find in Rome. There was no actual center to the cosmopolis, only a conceptual center — and precisely for this reason it was one that could be and was replicated in many different places" (Pollock 2006: 270).

While many scholars of cultural diffusion focus their attention on how outside ideas and norms transform existing beliefs and practices, the experience of Indianization in classical Southeast Asia suggests that ideational transmission is also about how it could lead to the *amplification* and *universalization* of local ideas and practices. As we

---

[7] Pollock defines "vernacularization" as "the historical process of choosing to create a written literature, along with its complement, a political discourse, in local languages according to models supplied by a superordinate, usually cosmopolitan, literary culture" (Pollock 2006: 23). As such, the concept complements and fits within the idea of localization.

have seen, van Leur argued that all external influences and foreign
ideas (whether Hindu, Buddhist or later Islamic), remained weak
and "did not bring about any fundamental changes in any part of
Indonesian social and political order" (van Leur 1955: 95). Wolters
argues that Hindu ideas did not transform Southeast Asian political
organization, but merely amplified the authority of the ruler. Hindu
ideas and practices "brought ancient and persisting indigenous
beliefs into sharper focus" (Wolters 1982: 9). Even after Hindu
ideas amplified their status and authority, indigenous beliefs such as
soul stuff and prowess "remained dominant" (Wolters 1982: 102).
"The 'Hindunized' polities were elaborations or amplifications of
the pre-'Hindu' ones." (Wolters 1982: 103) In the Philippines, the
Christian Holy Week was adapted and construed in terms of the
Tagalog concept of *loob*, implying "an inner self and a force with
power to attract followers" (Wolters 1982: 60). While Christian
missionaries did not want their self-purification rites to glorify and
amplify the indigenous concept of *loob* that underscores the "creative"
energy of the universe, but this is exactly what happened (Wolters
1982: 60). Localization did not lead to disappearance of existing
beliefs and practices. Instead, the latter were amplified. Foreign
ideas were used to enhance the status and legitimacy of local actors,
but they were rarely accepted in their pure form. They were used
to express local ideas, amplify them, and to pursue local interests.
Southeast Asian rulers constructed Indian notions of devotionalism to
enhance their legitimacy. The introduction of foreign ideas did not
lead to disappearance of existing local beliefs and practices. Rather,
the latter continued, albeit finding new modes of expression, and
were sometimes amplified. Thus, the institution of monarchy was
enhanced as, "soul stuff", already denoting innate spiritual energy,
was amplified with Indian divine mysticism, and "prowess" was
amplified when Southeast Asian rulers used Indian deities such as
Siva to claim legitimacy. An example of how these rulers used Hindu

concept to amplify their authority could be found in Cambodia as well as Chinese influenced Vietnam. In Cambodia, Wheatley argues that "it was because the grace of Siva was all pervasive that the populace submitted willingly to authority" (Wheatley 1982: 20).[8] In seventh century Cambodia, King Jayavarman I was said to be a "portion" of Siva, while Bhavavarman was said to have used Siva's *sakti* or divine energy to "seize the kingship" (Wolters 1982: 10). Vietnamese ruler Tran Thai-ton in 1258 sought to protect his polity from the Mongol invasion by assuming the name of the ancient Chinese ruler and sage Yao. He also nominated an heir even when he was still in his prime. This mimicked a similar move by Yao, which had attracted the praise of the Chinese sage Mencius. This way the king could establish a parallel with the Chinese rulers (Wolters 1982: 64). Analyzing poetry, Cambodian inscriptions and Khmer art (bas-reliefs in Angkor Wat), Wolters argues that Indian symbols had a "decorative" role; they were used to highlight the power and authority and the exalted position of the king and the golden age of his rule, and that they were "signifiers" which "were being employed in this [Cambodian] society to express important local ideas" (Wolters 1982: 89). Indian art was used to send the message that "the king was the source of creative and life-sustaining authority in Cambodia" (Wolters 1982: 89).

---

[8] Amplification can mean using foreign formats to describe local substance. For example, the Hindu manual of the Laws of Manu identified 18 points of litigation. This was used in Java where some of the laws were modified to accommodate Javanese customary law without altering the number 18 (Wolters 1982: 42). Beginning in thirteenth century, Vietnamese historians used Chinese imperial-history formats as a model for writing Vietnamese history. But the important thing is that while it was a Chinese format, the substance was Vietnamese (Wolters 1982: 42–3).

The localization of foreign ideas goes hand-in-hand with the universalization of local ones. One example of this type of change has been suggested by Kirsch in his study of Thai religion. Analysing the interaction between pre-existing Thai religious beliefs and the emergent Hinduism and Buddhism, Kirsch describes a process whereby indigenous spirits were identified with aspects of Hindu and Buddhist cosmology (for an illustration see the Thai spirit house with Siva lingams in the photo section) and beliefs through the "twin processes of parochialization and universalization".

> A locality spirit might be identified with a more abstract Hindu-Buddhist entity like Mae Thorani, the goddess of the earth. Initially, such identifications of indigenous spirits with more abstract religious entities would involve a degree of parochialization. By conceptually identifying a proximate and familiar spirit with a deity in a complex, abstract, universal cosmology, the deity is made less abstract and more on par with the indigenous system of beliefs. But such identifications simultaneously involve a process of universalization. The familiar spirit, now identified with a more abstract and universal cosmological scheme, is upgraded to an entity more distant than previously" (Kirsch 1977: 263).

The localization of Indian religion thus served local needs and purpose. The identification of indigenous spirits with Indian divinities meant that the existing conceptions of relationships between indigenous spirits were made more "explicable in terms of abstract concepts such as *karma* or more popular beliefs about merit." The resulting localization amplified, rather than extinguished existing practices and beliefs. At the same time, localization was not simply co-habitation of different beliefs that did not lead to change in local practices. Rather it created a "more complex and systematic order of relations between indigenous entities and beliefs" (Kirsch 1977: 263).

> The parochialization of Buddhist cosmology and belief might make it easier to spread Buddhism in initial contacts. But the attendant

universalization of indigenous beliefs could only serve to transform the religious scene, making it more complex and differentiated than it had been previously" (Kirsch 1977: 264).

Kirsch describes the change as "upgrading", a Parsonian phrase that suggests evolutionary transformation of an existing social and political system as a result of contact with a foreign influence. I would call it progressive transformation; "the Thai adoption of Theravada Buddhism ... facilitated the spread of Buddhism among the Thai peoples, and simultaneously transformed their religious and social system" (Kirsch 1977: 264). Bosch, who supported van Leur's "Idea of the Local Initiative", also suggests that the cultural and ideational interaction between India and Southeast Asia led to transformation and progress: "The foreign culture gradually blended with the ancient native one so as to form a novel, harmonious entity, giving birth eventually to a higher type of civilization than that of the native community in its original state" (Bosch 1961: 3).

Kirsch's framework is notable for it allows for the possibility of outside ideas adjusting to indigenous beliefs and practices as much as the local actors adapting to external ideas. Thus, the impact of foreign ideas on local settings need not be viewed as a one-way street. When a local system is "universalized," it may lead not only to the spread of the foreign idea that was responsible for the transformation of the local society, but also to a better projection of the indigenous beliefs within and beyond the local society. It can also open up the possibility that outsiders may develop a better understanding of local practices and may even borrow from them. Localization could thus become a two-way street. The two ideational structures (foreign and local) are thereby mutually-constituted. Universalization thus acquires a broader meaning. As Wolters put it, the infusion of foreign ideas into a local setting could have an outcome in which both the "local and foreign elements were 'universalized' and 'parochialized' respectively"

(Wolters 1982: 53). Their adaptation occurs over "long periods of time when both local and foreign elements were changing" (Wolters 1982: 53)[9] The agency for civilizational cultural and political advancement belongs to both foreign and local agents.

This leads to the idea of convergence proposed by Kulke in lieu of the Indianization thesis. In developing a critique of Indianization, Kulke notes:

> The concept of Indianization may help us to explain the way Indian influences initially spread to Southeast Asia, their Indian provenance, their agents etc. However it does not explain the quick and truly congenial advancement of Indian cultural traits in Southeast Asia. On the contrary, the very concept of Indianization prevents the understanding of the overall "process of civilization" in Southeast Asia and therefore, in some regards, the concept of Indianization may even have to be regarded as a misnomer in the context of Southeast Asia. (Kulke 1964: 13)

In contrast, the term "convergence" describes a two-way process:

> Unlike the Indianization concept the convergence hypothesis not only tries to give more space to indigenous initiatives in Southeast Asia. (sic) Moreover it tries to interpret the developments in early Southeast Asia in the framework of an overall historical process which includes and affected the societies of South and Southeast Asia as a whole. According to this hypothesis, it was the socio-economic and political convergence in both regions during the early centuries AD which required and enabled similar solutions to similar problems of social change. Whereas Indianization presumes social distance as a major cause of acceptance of Indian influences in Southeast Asia, the

---

[9] This outcome of localization of foreign ideas applied not just to the spread of Indian concepts, but could also be seen in the context of the spread of Chinese influence in Vietnam and Christian influence in the Philippines.

convergence hypothesis postulates social nearness as the promoter of social change under — undoubtedly — Indian influences in Southeast Asia. (Kulke 2006: 13–14)

Kulke argues that it was the contact and the affinity between South and Eastern India rather than Northern India which influenced the political development of Southeast Asia, as they were in similar stages of social and political development, in contrast to the more developed empires of North India. "For obvious reasons this Hindu model of a limited universal kingship was initially taken over by early local rulers of Southeast Asia from the princely states of South and Eastern India and not from the truly imperial Guptas of Northern India, and certainly not from the imperial court of China — a model that did not at all fit the requirements of contemporary Southeast Asia. Brahmins and scribes who brought the so-called Pallava Grantha script to Indonesia in about 400 CE were thus not emissaries of powerful Hindu rulers of South India (where indeed *no* powerful empires existed at that time). They came rather from princely courts whose rulers were still facing quite similar problems of establishing their authority and "domesticating" their people" (Kulke 1964: 13).

Kulke concludes that Indian ideas and culture did not arrive in Southeast Asia through "transplantation". Rather, it did so through a "complicated network of relations" (here Kulke uses de Casparis's words) in which India and Southeast Asia were "partners of mutual 'process of civilization' which comprised both sides of the Bay of Bengal" (Kulke 2006: 13). His idea of convergence is similar to that of localization, but advances on it by drawing parallels between Southeast Asian societies and the emerging states of South and Eastern India, allowing for both separate but a more interactive development of both.

The ideas of "localization" and "convergence" as discussed here offer yet another reason to challenge Huntington's "clash of civilizations" thesis. Huntington uses the phrases "de-Westernization" and "indige-nization" of elites (Huntington 1996: 76, 93, 94) to describe the tendency of elites who had contacts abroad (such as a Western education) to retreat into their local religious or cultural values once they return home. This widens the cultural gulf between developing countries and the West. The experience of the diffusion of Indian culture and ideas into Southeast Asia, in which Southeast Asians actively borrowed and modified Indian ideas, suggest that such indigenization or localization would produce a convergence (to be discussed later) of cultures rather than conflict.

4

UNDERSTANDING HOW AND WHY IDEAS SPREAD

In exploring the correlation between history and political science with respect to the diffusion of "ideas," I have used Goldstein and Keohane's notion of ideas without adopting their rationalist perspective (Goldstein and Keohane 1993). Goldstein and Keohane present a three-fold typology of ideas: as world views, principled beliefs, and causal beliefs (Goldstein and Keohane 1993: 8–11). World views "define the universe of possibilities for action" (Goldstein and Keohane 1993: 9). The world's religions constitute a major source of such ideas, while another example is the concept of sovereignty. Principled beliefs are "normative ideas that specify criteria for distinguishing right from the wrong and just from unjust" (Goldstein and Keohane 1993: 9). Such ideas are represented by the anti-slavery movement, or the more recent anti-land mines movement. Causal beliefs are "beliefs about cause-effect relationships which derive authority from the shared consensus of recognized elites, whether they are village elders or scientists at elite institutions" (Goldstein and Keohane 1993: 10). Such beliefs include scientific discoveries about the causes of disease, or the link between shared beliefs and revolutionary political change. One example which is especially relevant here is the time-honored idea of "consensus" (*mufakat*) in dispute settlement mechanisms in rural Indonesia, in which village elders guide a process of consultations that defines the parameters of a settlement. This reflects the causal idea that social order depends on the shared beliefs in the social organization of the village.

How does the above classification of ideas apply to the historio-graphical debates about the spread of Indian ideas to Southeast Asia? The kind of Indian ideas that found acceptance in Southeast Asia fall into what Goldstein and Keohane would call "world views," especially since they were directly or indirectly rooted in Hindu and Buddhist religious philosophies and traditions. But it is not possible to separate religion from politics in classical Southeast Asia, and there are clear overlaps between world views and other categories of ideas. As Goldstein and Keohane note: "Causal beliefs imply strategies for the attainment of goals, themselves valued because of shared principled beliefs, and understandable only within the context of broader world views" (Goldstein and Keohane 1993: 10). Similarly, many ideas, whether they relate to sovereignty, authority and legitimacy link all three types of ideas: "Doctrines and movements often weave con-ceptions of possibilities and principled and causal ideas together into what may seem to be a seamless web" (Goldstein and Keohane 1993: 11).

The Indian ideas that were transmitted to Southeast Asia included all three types, although most have their basis in religious tradition (Hindu-Buddhist). For example, Indian law texts, such as Manu's *Manusmrti*, (The Code of Manu) the most influential Indian legal text in Southeast Asia, is essentially a collection of normative prescriptions and proscriptions. The doctrine of *Dhamma* of the Indian emperor Ashoka, whose conversion to Buddhism served as a springboard for the spread of Buddhism beyond India, including Southeast Asia (Thambiah 1976), contained specific prohibitions against unjust and cruel treatment of human beings and animals. These are examples of principles beliefs. Similarly, the prime example of causal beliefs would be the *Arthasastra* of Kautilya, which influenced Southeast Asian statecraft, strategy and diplomacy. This book offered the ruler a wealth of ideas about how to preserve and expand his power. Thus, Indianization can be seen as a broad process that did "weave conceptions of possibilities and principled and causal ideas together into what may seem to be a seamless web" (Goldstein and Keohane 1993: 11).

Beyond the typology of ideas, the foregoing discussion of the diffusion of ideas in classical Southeast Asia has several major implications for the study of their diffusion across civilizations. The followingare especially important.

The first concerns the relationship between power and the transmission of ideas. Ideas have causal power and this causal power does not depend on conquest or coercion. The fact that Southeast Asian rulers used Indian ideas for legitimizing their power also suggests that power is constituted by ideas and the exercise of power can only be understood by looking at its ideational and inter-subjective basis. The Indianization process in Southeast Asia clearly highlights the distinction between voluntary adaptation and coerced introduction of foreign ideas into a local setting, capturing a dynamic vastly different from the theory of hegemonic socialization proposed by some scholars of international relations.

To elaborate, the flow of ideas and culture across the Bay of Bengal was crucial in shaping the political transformation of Southeast Asia. It helped the emergence of stronger states in Southeast Asia, strengthened the rulers' legitimacy and shaped their conduct of international relations. This important and independent role of ideas should thus be looked at first when analyzing the international politics of the Southeast Asian region. Yet, the spread of Indian ideas did require the force of hegemonic material power. In dismissing the Indian colonization of Southeast Asia thesis, van Leur and many other historians established that the Indian ideational penetration of Southeast Asia was done not through the exercise of coercive power (e.g. Indian conquest or colonization of Southeast Asia), but through cultural intercourse based on equality and reciprocity. George Coedès, a major figure in classical Southeast Asian scholarship, underscores this point by contrasting Indian and Chinese influence on Southeast Asia. In his view, the fact that China's cultural influence on Southeast Asia (except in the delta of Tongking in Northern Vietnam) was less pronounced compared to that of India could be attributed to radically different modes of interaction. "The exchanges of embassies between the two shores of the Bay of Bengal were made on the basis of equality, while the Chinese always demanded that the 'Southern Barbarians' acknowledge Chinese suzerainty by the regular sending of tribute" (Coedès 1968: 34). While this view may be questioned for overstating the coercive nature of Chinese influence in areas of Southeast Asia other than Vietnam, it does underscore some of the differences in Indian and Chinese influences on Southeast Asia. Bosch describes Indian influence as being of a "a theoretical and scholastic character, elements which remind us of manuscript, the code of law, the recluse's cell, the monastery, and which undoubtedly are just as incomparable with an environment of warriors or traders as they are in harmony with an intellectual sphere: with the classes of scribes, scholastics, initiates in the holy scriptures and legal systems" (Bosch 1961: 11). This presents an alternative ontology to contemporary realist theory and the Hegemonic Stability Theory in international relations literature, which remain wedded to an implicit belief that influence is a top-down process in which the most powerful state or states can impose their own norms and ideology over the weak.[1]

A second insight of this study is that ideas do not enter into a cultural or normative vacuum. The diffusion of ideas depends on their local reconstruction or potential and suitability for local reconstruction. Moreover, external ideas/norms do not extinguish

---

[1] Criticising hegemonic stability theory, Keohane argues that "The dominance of a single great power can contribute to order in world politics, in particular circumstances, but it is not a sufficient condition and there is little reason to believe that it is necessary" (Keohane 1984: 46). On further elaboration and critique of Hegemonic Stability Theory, (see Snidal 1985). Contrary to this thesis, Sardesai has argued that Indian ideas proved popular precisely because there was no direct political or strategic ambition on the part of India to dominate Southeast Asia. He too contrasts Indian and Chinese influence. The latter was often in the form of political intervention; but that might be why Chinese political ideas never got accepted in Southeast Asia; while it is "the relative lack of Indian political ambition in the region", along with greater commercial linkages and proximity, which produced widespread acceptance of India ideas (Sardesai 1994: 16). This has important implications for international relations scholarship which holds that hegemonic power is important to transmission of norms. In contemporary Southeast Asia, one finds the diffusion of the cooperative security idea was possible in the 1990s because the initiative for it came not from the major powers, but from middle and weaker powers such as Canada, Australia and ASEAN. Chinese officials have since made it clear that they would not have agreed to accept that idea and join the ASEAN Regional Forum (ARF) if the proposal had come from the U.S.; it was ASEAN's initiative that made a multilateral institution based on the cooperative security idea acceptable to China (Acharya 2009*a*, 2009*b*).

pre-existing local beliefs and practices, but may instead amplify them. On this point, it is worth stressing the point of most of the revisionist historians that Southeast Asia was not a clean slate into which foreign (Indian or Chinese) ideas and culture arrived — "a blank page on which Indians inscribed their alien signatures" (Wheatley 1982: 27). Instead, much of the revisionist literature assumes an "indigenous substratum" upon which the "superstructure" of Indian and Chinese cultural influences were erected (Sardesai 1994: 13).[2] Wilhelm Solheim pictures Southeast Asians as cultural and civilizational pioneers; before the arrival of Indians, many Southeast Asian innovations existed and had been transmitted to parts of China, Japan, and Indian Ocean coastal areas by Southeast

---

[2] Indeed, some scholars have argued that Southeast Asians gave as much as they learnt from foreign cultures and civilizations, although much of the occurred when foreigners arrived and settled in Southeast Asia and adapted local customs and practices. Evidence of cultural feedback from Southeast Asia to India, especially in economic and political matters, is scant. Southeast Asians did maintain cultural contacts, coming to study in Nalanda. The rulers of Srivijaya sent missions to the Pala kings in Bengal. A Nalanda inscription informs that Balaputradeva, a Srivijayan king around the AD mid-ninth century, asked the Pala king Devapala for land on which to build a monastery in Nalanda and was granted the request. Srivijayan rulers also donated gifts to the Chola kingdom in southern India, including financing a Buddhist monastery at Nagapattinam. These gifts, including gold and precious stones to temples, were supposedly meant to foster commercial ties between Srivijaya and the Chola kingdom (Sen 2009: 67). There is much more evidence of cultural feedback in the case of Greek influence over the Mediterranean, to be discussed later in this book, where Egyptian, Phoenician, Persian and Arabic ideas influenced Greece, which has been otherwise seen as the main idea giver of the Mediterranean.

Asian traders and sailors (Solheim 1971). These innovations included rice cultivation, bronze production, language elements, ideographs, outrigger canoes, iron and iron technology, etc. (Mabbett 1977*a*: 5–8). Wolters' notion of "soul stuff" offers an example of a pre-existing concept for political legitimization in Southeast Asia before the arrival of Indian culture. In a recent synthesis of new archaeological research on Southeast Asia's past, O'Reilly argues that the appearance of the Dong Son drums and jars "in many diverse parts of mainland and island Southeast Asia provides evidence [not only] of a sophisticated exchange network … at an early time" (meaning pre-Indic), but also of political connections, as the drums "probably served as symbols of authority, conferred upon other regional chiefdoms as emblems of power" (O'Reilly 2007: 39–40). It is because of this substratum that in the subsequent flow of Indian cultural styles, the Southeast Asian elite enjoyed a shared "cultural vocabulary" (O'Reilly 2007: 190).

But it may be the case that this pre-existing substratum or what may be called the "cognitive prior" (Acharya 2009*b*: 21–23) was not wholesome and offered no basis for durable political structures. In an elegant summary of the relevant evidence concerning Indian influence, Mabbett points to archaeological evidence that has led some scholars to argue that well before the arrival of Indians and Chinese, Southeast Asia already possessed "most of the attributes of civilization" and even "pioneered" many of them. What was missing, however, was "stratified societies and political centralization" (Mabbett 1977: 2). This is precisely where Indian ideas fitted in and made most of their mark. This not only attests to the importance of political ideas in the cultural transmission process, but also shows that new foreign ideas (in this case political ideas about kingship and authority) seldom enter a political and an ideational vacuum, but are instead filtered through the prism of an existing local framework, and accepted when they fit or can be made to fit, that existing framework.

Third, in order to be acceptable, foreign ideas must not only be suitable to local contexts, but should also amplify local beliefs and practices. To be sure, the adoption of foreign ideas depends on local need, especially political need. Indigenous structures, including the organization of power within the receiving state, determine which foreign ideas are appealing and thus to be adopted and which one are not. Thus, one of the reasons why Indian ideas found accept-ance in Southeast Asia might have had to do with "the absorptive, syncretic quality of Indian culture, itself enriched by numerous strands imported by a series of invaders of the Indian subcontinent" (Sardesai 1994: 16), which suited the cultural diversity of Southeast Asia. The hierarchical nature of classical Indonesia states was suited for the borrowing of those foreign cultural and political ideas (and the Indian ideas were perfect for this purpose) which supported and legitimised that hierarchy. Thus, the "process of Indianization should not be seen as simply involving a Southeast Asian acceptance of Indian cultural values". While, "Indian culture was absorbed in much of Southeast Asia, and Indian religions, art forms, and theories of government came to be of the greatest importance", this was because "it fitted easily with existing cultural patterns and religious beliefs." (Osborne 1979: 24–25).

A corollary to the above is that outside ideas and norms have a better chance of acceptance if they conformed to, or were consistent with, local norms and social practices. Local norms and practices provide the basis for deciding which outside ideas would be accepted or rejected. If an outside idea or norm is inconsistent with local needs or culture, it may be either rejected or adjusted. Outside ideas have a greater chance of being accepted if and when they address local deficiencies, rather than replacing existing forms. Southeast Asia was not devoid of political forms and institutions before

Indian influence arrived. The pre-existing form was based on rule by "man of prowess" using personal legitimacy rather than kinship-based ties. The kinship was "cognatic kinship" marked by relative indifference toward lineage descent. The lack of emphasis on lineage descent meant that other concepts and approaches of legitimacy were needed. This is precisely what Indian ideas of devotional legitimacy offered. They filled a gap.

Fourth, congruence between foreign and local ideas is to be understood not as a static fit, but as a dynamic condition. Neither is congruence to be seen as a response on the part of the recipients in adjusting indigenous beliefs to emerging ideas, the process could also move in the reverse direction, meaning their emerging ideas and norms could be accepted or rejected on the basis of their suitability for local reconstruction. Southeast Asians rejected many Indian ideas and practices which conflicted with local tradition and which could not be adapted. They "borrowed only those Indian and Chinese cultural traits that complemented and could be adapted to the indigenous system" (McCloud 1995: 69).

Fifth, foreign ideas do not necessarily penetrate all levels of the receiving society nor do they extinguish pre-existing local beliefs and practices. Ideational influence is never total or overwhelming; existing and traditional ideas and norms remain resilient. The most extreme proponent of this view is van Leur, who suggests that because of the selective nature of the borrowing of ideas by a small Southeast Asian elite, the traditional pre-existing and indigenous Indonesian culture and ideas survived through the spread of Indian ideas. The latter "did not bring about any fundamental changes in any part of Indonesian social and political order". While one might question van Leur's categorical assertion, as we have already noted, that the impact of Indian ideas on Southeast Asia were but "a thin and flaking glaze" (van Leur

1955: 95), the more pertinent claim here concerns the resilience of indigenous ideas alongside foreign ones. "In surveying the Indonesian forms one is constantly struck by the survival and strength of the traditional indigenous organizational forms, by the clear and colourful configurations wherever other forms by might and main (sic) superimposed themselves on the existing ones and under the tension of new adjustments created a new pattern, and by the durability of the forms when transferred outside Indonesia" (van Leur 1955: 102).

Finally, a study of the India-Southeast Asia relationship tells us that while ideas can spread through a process of social and cultural interaction, this need not be apolitical or non-rational. There is an element of strategic intent on the part of the both the givers and recipients. This has implications for one of the most important points of debate and synthesis in the contemporary understanding of why ideas and norms are borrowed and how they spread across cultures and international systems.

To elaborate, some scholars, like Goldstein and Keohane, take a rationalist view of the transmission and impact of ideas. For them ideas might be borrowed if they "affect strategic interactions," and help "efforts to attain 'more efficient' outcomes" (Goldstein and Keohane 1993: 12). At the opposite end, the social constructivist perspective stresses the moral purpose and constitutive impact of ideas. Ideas are borrowed because they support the recipients' need for moral and political legitimation. Actors accept ideas, build institutions around them and behave accordingly, not because ideas act as tools of utility and efficiency in a strategic interaction setting, but because these ideas and the behaviour they shape are understood to be good, desirable and appropriate. While the rationalist perspective on ideas stresses coercion, bargaining and compromises, the constructivist perspective centres on socialization, compliance, and transformation. In other words, the rationalist understanding of how ideas and norms spread is associated with a behavioral logic emphasizing utility maximization. Most constructivists have embraced the contrasting "logic of appropriateness" in which actors internalize norms "not for instrumental reasons — to get what they want — but because they understand the behavior to be good, desirable and appropriate" (Finnemore and Sikkink 1998: 912).

The initial rationalist-constructivist debate over ideas and their impact has led to a synthesis. From the syncretic perspective, the spread of ideas is seen to be driven by both strategic motivations, such as material self-interest, and normative considerations, including the desire for legitimation. This perspective holds that "instead of opposing instrumental rationality and social construction, we need to find some way to link those processes" (Finnemore and Sikkink 1999: 270). The spread of Indian ideas into Southeast Asia offers a powerful classical point of reference for such a synthetic approach to understanding the spread of ideas and norms that modern political scientists and international relations scholars can look to for their own work.

Out of the social and cultural interaction between India and Southeast Asia, the Brahmanas received material benefits while the kings secured and enhanced their legitimacy. Van Leur's thesis on "local initiative", as noted earlier, drew heavily from Weberian rationalism; Weber had argued in the Indian context that "the strongest motive for the assimilation of Hinduism was undoubtedly the desire for legitimation" (Weber 1920:18) and that for its recipients, Hindunization "secured their superiority over the subject classes with an efficiency unsurpassed by any other religion" (Weber 1958: 16). Yet, the process through which Indian religion and ideas spread was one not of coercion or conquest, but of social and cultural interaction. Moreover, the motive was not entirely rational need, or utility maximization. Prestige also played an important role.[3] Thus, this view of the spread of ideas falls somewhere in between the strategic interaction model favoured by rationalists on the one hand and the social interactionist model proposed by the constructivists on the other.

The diffusion of Indian culture and ideas into Southeast Asia was not a matter of "ideas all the way down." The existence of competing theories of Indianization suggests that material concerns, power

---

[3] Prestige plays an important role in the transmission of ideas. "Beliefs, fashions and manners may spread from one group to another without much regard to their intrinsic qualities. The group which adopts them may do so not because they satisfy some already existing need, but simply because they come from a group enjoying higher prestige. Stiff collars, long trousers and waistcoats are certainly not worn by inhabitants of the tropics because of any intrinsic merits of this attire. Religions, notions of honour and propriety, even political ideologies are often embraced regardless of their effects upon the structure of the society involved, simply because they come from a source enjoying higher prestige" (Andreski 1969: 180–81). The importance of prestige is certainly evident in the transmission of language. Gonda shows that linguistic borrowing in Indonesia from Indian Sanskrit was not always based on necessity. Sanskrit words were borrowed by Indonesians even when native expressions of the same ideas were available. This was because Sanskrit words enjoyed a higher prestige, and desire on the part of the natives to "imitate more civilized or prominent people." For example, the Malay term for husband is *suami*, (in Sanskrit *suamin*, meaning master, lord, king, husband), instead of the indigenous term *laki*, which is considered less respectful (Gonda 1973: 611).

and interest were not entirely irrelevant.[4] The idea of local initiative developed by van Leur, however attractive it might have been, had to be seen against the backdrop of alternative theories, such as trade and conquest. Trade, and the obvious material motives associated with it, deserves particular notice (the evidence of conquest is too sketchy).[5] Nonetheless, ideas defined a major part of the interaction between India and Southeast Asia and they helped to transform the political landscape of Southeast Asia. This supports Finnemore and Sikkink's idea of a "strategic social interaction" model, which they describe as a situation in which "actors are making detailed means-end calculations to maximize their utilities, but the utilities they want to maximize involve changing the other players' utility function in ways that reflect the normative commitments of norm entrepreneurs" (Finnemore and Sikkink 1999: 270). From the work of the historians of Southeast Asia, it is possible to discern various forms of interaction which I would call "strategic localization."

---

[4] One must note the material incentive of the moral entrepreneurs, the Brahmins. "At his court one sees many ... Brahmins who came from India to profit from his munificence and are much in his favour": this observation by the sixth century Chinese traveller Ma Tuan-lin of Brahmins in the royal court of a Malay coastal state captures the mutually beneficial relationship between the recipients and transmitters of Indian culture and political ideas (van Leur 1955: 357).

[5] Even van Leur himself admits that trade is what brought the Southeast Asian rulers in contact with Indian Brahmins in the first place: "Southern India was the trading region of Indonesia. By means of trade, whether carried on as Indonesian shipping or through the intermediacy of Indian shipping, the Indonesian rulers and aristocratic groups came into contact with India ..." (van Leur 98). Hence cultural interaction and socialization linked to communications that had a more material basis, especially trade.

The "rational" aspect of classical Southeast Asia's intercourse with India, the "rational" nature of this intercourse is borne out by the fact that Southeast Asians were not passive recipients, but active borrowers, of Indian ideas. They sought out ideas which would be beneficial and rejected those which were deemed harmful. Ideas were borrowed when they suited the local milieu and when they advanced the interests of the ruler. The "idea of the local initiative", as we have seen, is clearly imbued with Weberian rationalism. McCloud speaks of a new understanding of Southeast Asia's interaction with the outside world in which "Southeast Asians borrowed only those Indian and Chinese cultural traits that complemented and could be adapted to the indigenous system" (McCloud 1995: 69).[6] Fisher writes that Southeast Asians have "abundantly demonstrated their capacity to absorb, and more important, to discriminate in what they absorb" (Fisher 1964: 776). Some Indian ideas, such as the caste system, never flourished in Southeast Asia, as Mabbett shows. If this is true, it puts the focus on the role of recipients, and on the demand side, rather than on moral entrepreneurs and the supply side. And it introduces a significant rationalist element of consideration and selection to what would otherwise be clearly seen as a social and culturally determinist dynamic.

The transmission of ideas in classical and contemporary Southeast Asia was thus a process in which selective borrowing, shaped by preexisting understandings and cultural frameworks, had a decisive

---

[6] "These various cultural gifts from India became Southeast Asian and in doing so changed their character. In some cases, moreover, quite fundamental features of Indian culture and society were not adopted" (Osborne 1979: 24–25).

role. In this process, the recipients played as much a role as the suppliers. From the above discussion, one gets a framework for understanding the transmission of ideas as a process consisting of three inter-related steps: (1) "local initiative", or pro-active borrowing of external ideas; (2) "localization", or modification of external ideas to suit local belief and practice; and (3) "amplification and universalization", or the process by which external ideas are used to amplify existing ideas and practices and project them as more universal and to secure greater legitimacy and support for them in the wider cultural milieu than where they were initially prominent.

Figure 1   How Ideas Spread

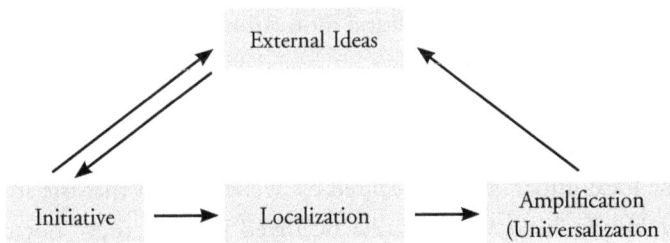

The foregoing analysis also permits two generalizations about how ideas spread: (1) that coercive power need not be a critical ingredient for the peaceful transmission of ideas; (2) that one of the most distinctive features of such non-hegemonic ideational interaction is the localization of outside ideas. This constitutes an alternative ontology in the international relations theory of ideas and norms. This perspective also challenges Huntington's "clash of civilizations" thesis. It shows that many clashes of ideas are settled through localization, rather than those ideas being in permanent contestation and conflict. Moreover, cultural interaction between nations, states and societies, does not involve a choice between good global (Western) norms and bad (non-Western, or Third World) local norms. Sometimes, regional actors want to persist with local beliefs and ideas about the conduct of social intercourse or international relations which enjoy considerable local legitimacy (not just cultural, but also on utilitarian grounds), but which may come into conflict with norms promoted by non-regional norm entrepreneurs, be they governments or members of a transnational civil society. In some such situations, local norms and practices might prevail, thereby severely restricting the impact of outside norms and ideas. In other cases, local actors may borrow selectively, and even pro-actively, from outside ideas and norms and even then, adapt or modify them to suit the local context, and infuse them with local ideas and practices.

Lastly, one can identify several motivations of why and how ideas spread.

1. *Efficiency and empowerment:* whether the foreign idea helps the borrower to achieve more efficient outcomes. Van Leur's "idea of the local initiative" was inspired by Weber's thesis that the spread of Hindu ideas within India occurred because they "not only endowed the ruling stratum ... with a recognized rank in the cultural world of Hinduism, but, through their transformation of castes, secured their superiority over the subject classes with an efficiency unsurpassed by any other religion" (Weber 1958: 16).

2. *Applicability:* whether the foreign idea fits the local context and whether it can be adapted. Southeast Asians seem to have been quite selective about which Indian ideas to borrow.

3. *Legitimation:* whether the foreign idea helps to legitimize an existing authority vis-à-vis relevant internal and external actors and environments. This was a key factor in the Southeast Asian rulers' receptivity to Indian religious and political ideas.

Some Indian secular ideas about statecraft, such as Kautilya's *Arthasastra,* empowered Southeast Asian rulers in a strategic sense; other Indian religious ideas were appealing because they helped to legitimize them.

4. *Universalization:* whether accepting a foreign idea helps to enhance the prestige and applicability of some local beliefs and practices in a wider context. This is central to Wolters' notion of "amplification" and Kirsch's notion of "Universalization."

5

"HELLENIZATION" OF THE MEDITERRANEAN COMPARED TO "INDIANIZATION" OF SOUTHEAST ASIA: TWO PARADIGMS OF CULTURAL DIFFUSION?

In defending his idea of "Sanskrit cosmopolis," Sheldon Pollock writes:

"The labels by which we typically refer to these earlier processes — Hellenization, Indianization, Romanization, Sinicization, Christianization, Islamization, Russification, and the like — are often used crudely and imprecisely. Yet they do serve to signal the historically significant ways in the past of being translocal, of participating — and knowing one was participating — in cultural and political networks that transcended the immediate community. These ways varied widely." (Pollock 2006: 10)

Another usefulness of these concepts is that they permit comparison across regional worlds. The importance of the spread of Indian ideas to Southeast Asia as a point of reference for the peaceful transmission of ideas can be better understood by comparing it with Hellenization, the other major case of the spread of ideas in classical history. There are a number of obvious parallels between the Indianization of Southeast Asia and the Hellenization of the Mediterranean. Broadly stated, Hellenization "refers to Greek culture and the diffusion of that culture" (Roberts 2007: 329).[1] Hellenization is often associated with the aftermath of Alexander's conquests, to the kingdoms founded by his generals: Ptolemy's in Alexandria and the Selucids in Antioch (in modern Syria). But Hellenization, in its broad sense of diffusion of Greek culture and influence, started in the eighth century BCE. (Jannelli and Longo 2004: 6). The first wave of Greek colonization was believed to have been between the eighth and sixth centuries BCE. It continued after the victories of Alexander, but it is important to understand that its origins predated Alexander's conquests. It was the offshoot of trade, but also of the migration of Greeks and the establishment of Greek "colonies" throughout the Mediterranean, western and eastern.

In both cases of Hellenization and Indianization, the term "colony" is used, but in both cases it connotes not colonialism in the modern sense of military conquest and occupation, but migration and settlement. But conquest was perhaps more true of the Greeks in the Mediterranean than the Indians in Southeast Asia. The term "colonia" or colony comes from the Latin *colere*, and was first employed by the Romans, "who used it describe groups of citizens to whom they gave land for the purpose of cultivation but who maintained

---

[1] Hellenization should not be conflated with the Hellenistic period which refers to the period between the death of Alexander the Great in 323 BCE and the victory of Octavian (Augustus) at Actium in 31 BCE (Roberts 2007: 329).

ties of various kinds with Rome" (Jannelli and Longo 2004: 6–7). The Greeks themselves called the new *poleis* in the Mediterranean *apoikia,* indicating separation. Similarly, while Indian historians like Majumdar used the term colony, or Indian colonization, they did not necessarily mean physical conquest followed by occupation, but migration of whole groups of Indians into Southeast Asia. *Apoikia* "meant that a group of citizens moved away and set up their homes elsewhere" (Olivia 1981: 85). Hence, colonization in one context refers to creation of city states, in other senses just physical migration. The former connotes a significantly greater degree of political activity than the latter. To be sure, the Greek colonies became independent of their mother city (Olivia 1981: 85–6), but still reproduced its institutional forms and practices to a great degree, despite some localization.

In this sense, Greek colonization around the Mediterranean and the Black Sea between the eighth and sixth centuries BCE can be compared with Indian colonization of Southeast Asia as interpreted by Majumdar. But there are major differences. One is the question of how large-scale the Indian exodus really was. Greeks certainly left home in massive numbers. Indian traders seemed to have been happy to return home after making their earnings. Greek colonists left because of economic hardship at home; their lands were infertile and resources scarce. The Indians who left their homes for Suvarnadwipa (island of gold) were relatively well-off merchants in search of economic opportunity, not driven by economic misery. According to folklore, the *Sadhava,* or merchant, from Kalinga who routinely embarked on voyages to Southeast Asia was from an affluent class, made more prosperous by the commerce. Some historians have suggested that the Kalinga War of 261 BC, in which Maurya Emperor Ashoka vanquished the independent kingdom of Kalinga (modern Orissa) on the Bay of Bengal coast led to a sizable exodus of the surviving Kalinga people to the eastern lands across the sea (Patra 2010: 19).[2] But the authenticity of this exodus cannot be confirmed, although there is greater evidence of the commercial voyages and emigration of Kalinga people, whose point of origin includes what is today Orissa as well as northern Andhra Pradesh, to Southeast Asia, and their cultural and economic presence especially in what are today Burma (Myanmar), Malaysia (where they are known as "klings"), Cambodia, and Indonesia.

Earlier understandings of the spread of Greek culture in the Mediterranean, like that of the spread of Indian culture in Southeast Asia, viewed the role of the local communities as passive. This was especially the case with the westward spread of Greek culture. John Boardman's seminal study of Greek migration contended that: "In the west the Greeks had nothing to learn, much to teach" (cited Hodos 2006: 11).[3] Criticizing Boardman, Hodos argues that for Boardman, "Greek culture (itself viewed as somewhat static), overwhelmed others with its sophistication of objects and artefacts, and enlightened customs and traditions ... there is little consideration of acts of agency on the part of the non-Greeks, nor of any reciprocity." (Hodos 2006: 11)

---

[2] According to an inscription of Maurya Emperor Ashoka (the thirteenth Rock Edict), the Kalinga War claimed 100,000 dead, while 150,000 were taken prisoner, and an indeterminate number perished from the war's after effects. Translation of the text of the edict in Thapar 1996: 255.

[3] In this respect, the experience of Hellenization in the eastern Mediterranean, particularly Asia Minor and Egypt, was quite different from the Hellenization of the western Mediterranean. Although in neither space the Greeks ideas are likely to have encountered a cultural vacuum, in the Eastern Mediterranean they encountered powerful pre-existing civilizations — Mesopotamia, Persia and Egypt and were greatly influenced by their ideas — including in areas such as religion and science.

But this was challenged in later historiography. The result is often termed "hybridity." As Hodos puts it, in the new historiography on Greek influence on the Mediterranean, "there has been an emphasis upon the new cultures that emerged out of colonial encounters, cultures that are a blend of indigenous and foreign traditions, actively reinterpreted into something new that is specific to a particular situation ... The focus of hybridity studies rests upon the active construction of local identities in contact situations ..." (Hodos 2006: 17). According to Hodos, "not all aspects of Greek culture were adopted by those with whom the Greeks came into contact through prolonged settlement, and different aspects were preferred by some and not others" (Hodos 2006: 11). Hodos criticizes the very concept of Hellenization on the grounds that "Its usage...implies a passive acceptance of Greek material goods and ideologies on the part of the non-Greeks, with no consideration of agency, nor of reciprocity" (Hodos 2006: 11).

This is the more common view now. In more recent literature, Hellenization is defined as an "active process." Roberts argues that "Often the eventual outcome [of the contact between Greek and preexisting cultures] was not so much the diffusion of Greek culture as the fusion of practices Greek and non-Greek" (Roberts 2007: 329).

We have seen that the earlier Indianization thesis was similarly critiqued and modified in the revisionist historiography of Southeast Asia. To some extent, the revisionist historiography of Hellenization mirrors the revisionist history of Indianization. Localization through the agency of local actors did occur in the Mediterranean, just as it did in Southeast Asia. But despite these similarities, Hellenization and Indianization differ in significant ways. Two are especially important. The first and most important is the role of violence, the second is the extent of local agency. Hellenization was marked by considerable violence and warfare, both between the Greeks and the preexisting communities, and between the different Greek colonists themselves. This involved rivalries and power politics, sometimes reproducing the rivalries among the Greeks city-states in their homeland. This was especially evident in Sicily, the first major site of Greek colonization in the Mediterranean:

> By this time [early seventh century BC), the first wave of Sicilian Greek colonists had realized the potential of Sicily for economic and political control, and the original colonies began to establish sub-colonies, creating alliance links and carving up the island into spheres of politico-military influence. Syracuse's foundation of Helorus, Akrai, Kasmenai and Camarina bound the south-east of the island to Syracusan control, while Gela's foundation of Akragas secured the south-western coast-line, as Zancle's establishment of Himera did for the northern coast. Megara Hyblaea's foundation of Selinus gave the Megarians their own foothold in western Sicily. Leontini founded the subcolony of Euboia, probably on the south-west margin of the Catania Plain at what is known today as Monte San Mauro di Caltagirone ... Thus the stage was set for the subsequent inter-Greek battles for territorial control, conflict that ultimately involved all peoples living on the island (Hodos 2006: 89–90).

Even if the spread of Greek ideas was initially pacific and was preced-ed by trade, the consolidation of Greek influence was accompanied by military conflict. Moreover, Greek colonization resulted in city states that were for the Greeks, by the Greeks and of the Greeks. "Greek colonization ... involved the foundation of new political communities, new *poleis* formed by groups of citizens disengaged from the original community, which was known to them as the *metropolei* ("the mother city"). They brought with them the language, religious and cultural traditions, and myths and institutions inherited from the original *polis*, but now totally independent of it ..." (Jannelli and Longo 2004: 6).

By contrast, the spread of Indian influence resulted in the estab-lishment of states and political institutions that were for the Southeast

Asians, by the Southeast Asians and of the Southeast Asians. Southeast Asians borrowed Indian ideas to legitimize themselves, consolidate their authority and control and organize their polities into larger kingdoms. But in essence, these kingdoms were ruled by the natives, not by Indians (despite occasional mythology about Indian sojourners founding kingdoms in Southeast Asia).

A second major difference between Hellenization and Indianization has to do with local initiative and agency. While the revisionist historiography of both claims significant local agency, it appears to have been greater in the case of Indianization. It should be noted that the term local or native is a misnomer for the Greek colonists in Sicily since the so-called natives — Sika, Sikel and Elymians — were from earlier and fairly recent migration from other parts of Mediterranean, especially the Italian peninsula. This local population did not call upon Greek culture to legitimize their rule, but faced the threat of extinction from the Greeks. There is also some evidence of alliances and collaboration between these groups and the Greeks, as various *poleis* in Sicily enlisted the help of the natives to fight rival *poleis*. Then there is the prominent example of the fifth century BC Sikel chief Ducezio, who founded a Sikel confederation against the Greeks of Agrigento. Upon defeat, he went into exile to Corinth, only to return with the support of the Corinthians (and perhaps with help from Syracuse) to establish a new city of Kalacte (Jannelli and Longo 2004: 10–11). We have no similar evidence of alliances formed by Indian migrants and native rulers, although this could be due to the paucity of archaeological and textual data. What in the case of Indianization has been termed "the idea of the local initiative" was probably missing or significantly lower in the case of Hellenization.

Another difference between the outward spread of Indian and Greek cultures may be noted. In the Mediterranean, we see that the colonizing Greeks accepted some aspects of the pre-existing local culture, especially local deities. But the Hellenization of some places in the western Mediterranean, especially Sicily, left very little trace of the pre-existing culture and identity of the local population. Hence, Freeman writes that "The Sikel could become a Greek yet more thoroughly than the Briton could become an Englishman" (Freeman 1891: 320). In the words of a narrative found at the exhibits of the Syracuse Museum:

> From the seventh century BCE onwards, the indigenous cultures are to be transformed by the contact with the Greeks, and the process of assimilation and acculturation will go on until the absorption of Greek culture by the natives, so that from the fifth century B.C. differences will be only economic rather than cultural.

This was in marked contrast to the spread of Indian culture in Southeast Asia. As we have seen, not only did the elements of the pre-existing local culture remain fairly visible, but they also modified or localized the foreign elements in accordance with indigenous culture and practice. The coasts of Sicily today are dotted with magnificent ruins of Greek temples modelled after those in parent city-states (albeit with some modifications), but we do not see replicas of Indian temples in Southeast Asia (with the possible exception of Burma, especially the Ananda Temple in Pagan, which has been likened to some temples of Bengal and Orissa in design). Notwithstanding the fact that the layout of Southeast Asian Hindu temples was based on the sacred Mount Meru and were undergirded by Indian conceptions of state and kingship (Heine-Geldern 1956), one finds, as many commentators have noted, there is no Angkor Wat, Borobudur or Bayon in India.

The fact that India and Greece (before Alexander) could exert such a profound influence on neighbouring societies despite not being major imperial powers is significant. In the pre-Alexander Greece, and for India more generally, migration, rather than conquest, might have been the chief means of the diffusion of ideas. But in one sense at least, the Indianization of Southeast Asia, without the backing of military conquest, left a more profound legacy than the Hellenization of the eastern Mediterranean and beyond that followed Alexander's conquests. This has to do with the fact that Hellenization weakened after the death of Alexander, especially in Asia Minor (including the Hellenistic rulers in Antioch), Persia and ultimately in Egypt. By contrast, Indian ideas remained influential in Southeast Asia right up to the fifteenth century CE.

In both regional worlds, the materially more powerful actor did not turn out to be the most powerful ideational influence. In the Mediterranean littoral itself, Greek ideas remained influential, even after the total eclipse of the Greek political order in the hands of Rome. While Rome ruled over many of the Hellenistic areas, including Athens and the Ptolemaic kingdom of Egypt, the Roman emperor Hadrian heavily embraced Greek culture. One might compare this with Alexander's own embracing of Egyptian concepts of universal monarchy, anointing himself as Pharaoh in Memphis near Alexandria on 14 November 332 BCE, thus becoming perhaps the first universal ruler in Western history. Alexander also had no difficulty worshipping the Egyptian deities, such as the Egyptian Amun, whom he regarded as a form of Zeus. In fact, Rome emerged as the biggest promoter of Greek ideas. Thus, in the Mediterranean world order, the more powerful actor adopted and used preexisting local symbols, concepts and practices to legitimize its political prestige and authority, including imperialism in the lands it had conquered by force.[4]

---

[4] A point to note here is that with Alexander the Great, Hellenization became a matter of conquest, rather than commerce or persuasion. From then on, Greek or Hellenistic ideas would spread by the sword and empire, quite different from the earlier phase of Greek diffusion which, despite

By contrast, in the case of Indianization, we mainly see local actors using foreign symbols, concepts and practices to promote their legitimacy, prestige and authority, and in some cases turn themselves into empires. This kind of ideational exchange also occurred in the case of Hellenization, but the main pattern was diffusion through direct Greek creation of the institution of the *poleis* (foreign Greeks diffusing and recreating — with some local variations — their own political institutions in lands they settled for their own benefit). The Indian experience in Southeast Asia was probably more comparable to some pacific aspects of Romanization, whereby local non-Roman rulers borrowed Roman ideas to boost their legitimacy, and to the practice of Roman rulers themselves who looked to Greece for ideas and symbols to enhance their political legitimacy and prestige. But overall Roman influence around the Mediterranean was established by the power of the sword, not by the power of culture or ideas.

While Greek ideas proved arguably as much, if not more, influential in the Mediterranean as the Roman ones, with Roman emperors and elites borrowing them for their own legitimation, in Southeast Asia, the ideational influence of India, including Hindu-Buddhist political and cultural concepts had a profound influence in state-making and intra-regional interactions, arguably eclipsing the ideational influence of China (except in the deltas of Tongking in Northern Vietnam), the materially and geopolitically more powerful actor. This variance between the impact of indic and siniz ideas could be attributed to radically different modes of interaction. To quote George Coedès, "The Chinese [in Vietnam] proceeded by conquest and annexation; soldiers occupied the country, and officials spread

---

the strategic rivalries among the Greeks and their many conflicts with the native population in the "colonies," was mainly through peaceful overseas migration.

Chinese civilization. Indian penetration or infiltration seems to have been mostly peaceful; nowhere was it accompanied by the destruction that brought dishonor to the Mongol expansion or the Spanish conquest of America. Far from being destroyed by the conquerors, the native peoples of Southeast Asia found in Indian society, transplanted and modified, a framework within which their own society could be integrated and developed" (Coedès 1968: 34). While Coedès wrote this to compare Indian and Chinese lagacies in Southeast Asia, it better describes the difference between the Hellenization of the Mediterranean and the Indianization of Southeast Asia.

To conclude, in comparing the Hellenization of the Mediterranean with the Indianization of Southeast Asia, one finds striking similarities but also major differences. The most important ideas influencing regional society and political matrixes were not those of materially hegemonic actors, namely Rome and China, but those of countries which possessed superior ideational resources: India and Greece. Rome imbibed Greek ideas to legitimize itself. China accepted Buddhism from India. But while Indianization and Hellenization played similar roles in their respective regions, they did not have similar trajectories. A key difference was that Indianization spread through peaceful means, while Hellenization was often a byproduct of competition, rivalry and conquest. Hence it is Indianization, rather than Hellenization, which offers a more substantial evidence of the power of ideas over the ideas of the powerful.

6

FINAL THOUGHTS

When civilizations encounter each other, they trigger one of the most powerful currents of social and political change known to humankind. Yet, these changes do not amount to a "clash of civilizations". As Peter Katzenstein notes, "Civilizations exist in the plural. They coexist with each other ..." (Katzenstein 2010: 2). In this essay, I have challenged the strategic view of the encounter among civilizations, a view initially offered by Samuel Huntington but which found a wide international audience in the wake of the 9/11 attacks and the global war on terror led by the United States. The insights from the flow of ideas between India and Southeast Asia show that the interaction among civilizations should be understood not just in material terms, but also in ideational ones. Analyzing such interactions through the lens of local initiative, localization and convergence demonstrates that the process of such inter-civilizational encounters can be pacific, and their outcome productive. Not only those who bring in the new ideas, but also those who borrow them, are often motivated by a desire for self-legitimation and universalization. The history of civilizations may thus be told not in terms of blood, treasure and conflict, but ideas, identity and mutual benefit.

PHOTO SECTION

Localization and Legitimation

The images section highlights different aspects of the diffusion of Hindu and Buddhist religious architecture and imagery to Southeast Asia. While not exhaustive, they speak to some of the key themes of the book, especially localization and legitimation. Readers from India or those familiar with Indian temples and divine images but new to Southeast Asian temple imagery will note the distinctiveness of the Southeast Asian forms.

Plates 1, 2, 3, 4 While Indian (Hinduism and Buddhism) in conception and architectural form, there are no known examples of these grand monuments of Southeast Asia in India itself, suggesting local agency and purpose, rather than wholesale importation of Indian designs and architectures. The pyramidal architecture of Borobudur suggests a Buddhist edifice erected on a pre-Indic megalithic foundation. As Quaritch Wales says: although Indian "both in conception and in architectural form," Borobudur also shows "locally-guided evolution". (Wales 1951: p. 121)

Plates 5, 6, 7, 8 Hinduism practiced in Bali, including temple rituals, differs in significant respects from that in India. Hooykaas has identified several features of Balinese Hinduism which are different from the Indian brand. These include the Balinese belief that one is reborn within one's groups of relatives, that gods normally live in mountains and lakes and not in temples, and that cremation should be performed only depending on one's social position. (Hooykaas p. 25, cited in Wolters 1982: 59)

Plates 9, 10 Despite keeping to its central characters, the Javanese version of *Ramayana* not only omits many aspects of the Valmiki *Ramayana* of India, but also introduces indigenous deities unrecognizable to Indians. As Wolters put it, the old Javanese *Ramayana* offers an example of "a foreign text — the famous Indian epic — [that was] extensively reworked in Java to enable to local elite to savour and perhaps recite it aloud." (Wolters 1999: 186). Among other things, the Indian version of the epic from which Javanese adapted their *Ramayana*, the *Bhattikavya*, was used as a model only for the first half of the Javanese poem. In the second half, the Javanese introduced Javanese indigenous deities, and "improvised a happy ending to the Rama story". (Wolters 1999: 186)

Plate 11 The Funeral of Ravana (Tosakan), Temple of the Emerald Buddha, Grand Palace, Bangkok, Thailand: The palace of *Ravana* (*Tosakan* in Thai), like all depictions of buildings in the mural paintings of *Ramayana* (Ramakian) at the temple, is traditional Thai style, rather than Indian, while the face images on the gate of Ravana's palace evokes the Bayon of Cambodia, a historic enemy of Siam.

Plate 12 Borobudur bas relief: "The wonderful bas-reliefs of the Borobudur (sic) the originality and freedom for which they are so justly famous are not merely a matter of local variation in the rendering of scenes from the Lalita Vistara and Jataka stories, the introduction of Javanese animals and plants, etc., ... they [also] find scope for expression in the sculptural technique itself. For although this must have been mainly learnt from India, the peculiar refinement and delicacy, on which all have remarked, probably in some degree reflect the ability that the Javanese had acquired when their megalithic forebears (sic) were learning to express themselves naturalistically under Han guidance." (Wales 1974: 122)

Plates 13, 14   The borrowing and localization of Hindu-Buddhist religion and political ideas might have been motivated by a ruler's desire and need for legitimation and to consolidate small chiefdoms into major states. In classical Southeast Asia, temples (both Hindu and Buddhist) had a major place in the organization of the state and role in the legitimation of the ruler's authority. Battle scenes depicted in bas reliefs had a significant legitimizing function, signifying the ruler's power and prestige.

Plate 15   Bayon, Cambodia, defaced Buddha. Religion and politics were inseparable in classical Southeast Asia. One example is the defacing of Buddha images and their superimposition by Hindu deities in Bayon.

Plate 16   Borobudur: Sudhana near Kutagara of Maitreya: In the original Indian script of Gandhavyuha, Sudhana is the son of a merchant, a commoner. But in Borobudur, he is presented as a royal-like figure, visiting Maitreya and other deities with regalia and military entourage. Julie Gifford argues that "By picturing Sudhana as a king leading a martial procession, the designers of Borobudur set up a homology between the Pilgrim who becomes a Bodhisattva and the Sailendra king ... If Borobudur sometimes served as the venue for Sailendra royal rituals, then the king's performance of the ritual would bring the homology to life and quite possibly be itself an exercise in ceremonial diplomacy." (Gifford 2011: 177–78)

Plate 19 The Mukhalinga, or the "face of the Linga", made it easier for rulers to seek legitimation. The representational human form of Shiva made it easier for a ruler to identify with Shiva, allowed to personalize his power, and distinguish the ruler from the pre-Indic past.

Plate 20 The sparsely decorated Po Rome Tower, one of the last to be built in Champa, signified the decline of the Champa civilization. The borrowing of Indian ideas declined and ended, and Champa return to simpler forms of architecture, contrast from the rich decorations of Towers like Po Klung Garai (rebuilt) in the earlier period.

Plate 21 Bas relief of the deified ruler Po Rome after whom the complex is named. He is portrayed as an incarnation of Siva.

Plate 22 The appearance of Kuts in the tower signify a return to the indigenous beliefs and practices after the outer layer of Indianization had faded, a trend that Paul Mus (funerary stones) has described as: "Almost all Cham cults show three stages: indigenous religion, application and assimilation of Hinduism, return to the indigenous." (cited in Wales 1951: 15)

Plate 1 Borobudur, Indonesia
Source: **Amitav Acharya**

Plate 2 Bagan, Myanmar

Plate 3 Angkor Wat, Cambodia
Source: **Amitav Acharya**

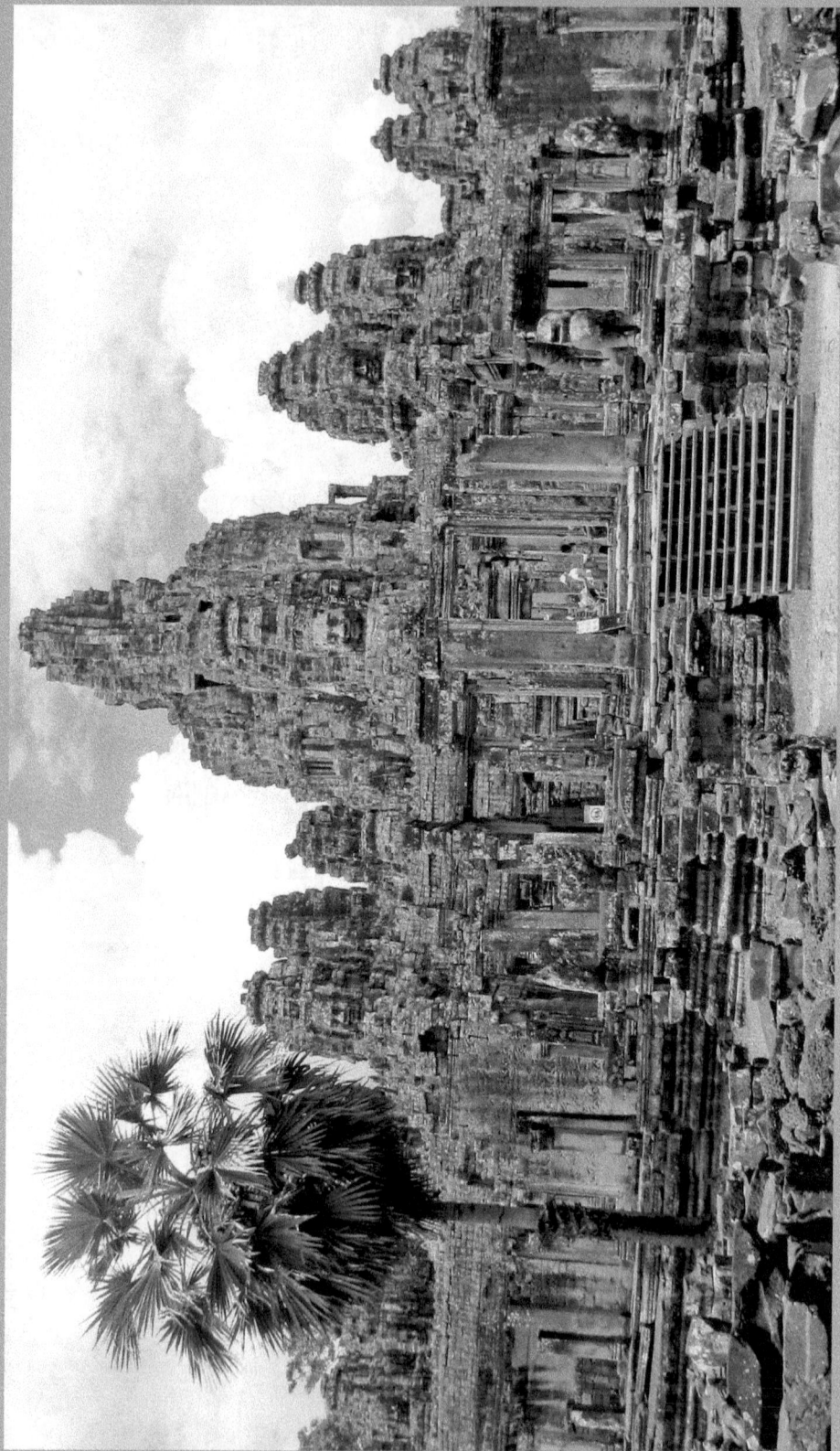

Plate 4 Bayon, Angkor Thom, Cambodia

Plate 5 A Balinese Hindu Temple
Source: **Amitav Acharya**

Plate 6 Mythical Figures in a Balinese Hindu Temple

Plate 7 A Balinese Priest
Source: **Amitav Acharya**

Plate 8 A Female Gamelan Band at a Balinese Temple
Source: **Amitav Acharya**

Plate 9 Prambanan Temple

Plate 10 Prambanan Relief: Rama and Laxman
Source: **Amitav Acharya**

Plate 11 The Funeral of Ravana (Tosakan), Temple of the Emerald Buddha, Bangkok, Thailand
Source: Amitav Acharya

Plate 12 Borobudur Bas Relief
Source: Amitav Acharya

Plate 13 Bayon, Angkor Thom: Relief of a Royal Procession
Source: Amitav Acharya

Plate 14 Bayon, Cambodia: Relief of Battle Scene – The Retreat of the Khmer Army from Cham Attack
Source: Amitav Acharya

Plate 15 Bayon, Angkor Thom, Defaced Buddha
Source: Amitav Acharya

Plate 16 Borobudur: Sudhana near Kutagara of Maitreya
Source: Amitav Acharya

Plate 17 Po Nagar Cham (Champa) Tower, Nha Trang, Vietnam
Source: **Amitav Acharya**

Plate 18 Po Klung Garai Cham Tower, Phan Rang (Panduranga), Vietnam

Plate 21 King Po Rome and his Queen, Po Rome Cham Tower, Vietnam
Source: **Amitav Acharya**

Plate 22 The Funerary Stones (Kut) at Po Rome Cham Tower
Source: **Amitav Acharya**

BIBLIOGRAPHY

Acharya, Amitav. 2000. *The Quest for Identity: International Relations of Southeast Asia.* Singapore: Oxford University Press.

———. 2006. Siva, Indochina and the Geopolitics of Peace, *Indian Express,* 29 September 2006. Available at <http://www.indianexpress.com/news/siva-indochina-and-the-geopolitics-of-peace/13572/0> (Accessed 20 November 2011).

———. 2009a. *Constructing a Security Community in Southeast Asia: ASEAN and the Problem of Regional Order* (2nd Edition). London and New York: Routledge.

———. 2009b. *Whose Ideas Matter: Agency and Power in Asian Regionalism.* Ithaca: Cornell University Press.

———. 2010. "Ideas, Norms and Regional Orders," Paper presented to the Conference on "When Regions Transform: Theory and Change in World Politics," McGill University, Montreal, Canada, 1–2 May 2010.

Anderson, Benedict. 1966. "The Languages of Indonesian Politics". *Indonesia,* vol. 1, pp. 89–116.

———. 1990. *Language and Power: Exploring Political Cultures in Indonesia.* Ithaca: Cornell University Press.

Basa, Kishor K. 1998. "Indian Writings on Early History and Archaeology of Southeast Asia: A Historiographical Analysis". *Journal of the Royal Asiatic Society of Great Britain & Ireland* (3rd Series), vol. 8, pp. 395–410.

Bekker, Konrad. 1951. "Historical Patterns of Cultural Contact in Southeast Asia". *Far Eastern Quarterly*, vol. 9, no. 1, pp. 3–15.

Benda, Harry. 1962. The Structure of Southeast Asian History: Some Preliminary Observations. *Journal of Southeast Asian History*, vol. 3, no. 1, pp. 106–38.

Bentley, G. Carter. 1985. "Indigenous States of Southeast Asia". *Annual Review of Anthropology*, vol. 76, pp. 275–305.

Boardman, John. 1999. *The Greeks Overseas*. London: Thames and Hudson.

Bosch, F.D.K. 1961. *Selected Studies in Indonesian Archaeology*. The Hague: Martinus Nijhoff.

Briggs, Lawrence P. 1948. "The Hinduized States of Southeast Asia: A Review". *Far Eastern Quarterly*, vol. 7, no. 4, pp. 376–93.

Cady, John F. 1964. *Southeast Asia: Its Historical Development*. New York: McGraw Hill.

Checkel, Jeffrey T. 1997. "International Norms and Domestic Politics: Bridging the Rationalist-Constructivist Divide". *European Journal of International Relations*, vol. 3, no. 4, pp. 473–95.

———. 1998. "The Constructivist Turn in International Relations Theory". *World Politics*, vol. 50, pp. 324–48.

Çoedès, George. 1964. "Some Problems in the Ancient History of the Hinduized States of Southeast Asia". *Journal of Southeast Asian History*, vol. 5, pp. 1–14.

———. 1968. *The Indianized States of Southeast Asia*. Hawaii: University of Hawaii Press.

Cortell, Andrew, and James Davis. 1996. "How Do International Institutions Matter? The Domestic Impact of International Rules and Norms". *International Studies Quarterly*, vol. 40, pp. 451–78.

Crawford, Neta. 1993. "Decolonization as an International Norm: The Evolution of Practices, Arguments, and Beliefs". In *Emerging Norms of Justified Intervention*, edited by Laura W. Reed and Carl Kaysen. Cambridge: American Academy of Arts and Sciences, pp. 37–61.

Cuff, E.C, E W.W. Sharrock and D. W. Francis. 1998. *Perspectives in Sociology* (4th Edition). London: Routledge.

De Casparis, J.G. 1983. *India and Maritime South East Asia: A Lasting Relationship*. Kuala Lumpur: University of Malaya Press.

De Saussure, Ferdinand. 1966. *Course in General Linguistics*. New York: McGraw Hill Book Company.

Du Bois, Cora. 1951. "The Use of Social Science Concepts to Interpret Historical Materials: Comments on the Two Preceding Articles". *Far Eastern Quarterly*, vol. 9, no. 1, pp. 31–34.

Finnemore, Martha, and Kathryn Sikkink. 1998. "International Norm Dynamics and Political Change". *International Organization*, vol. 52, no. 4, pp. 887–917.

Finnemore, Martha. 1996. "Norms, Culture and World Politics: Insights from Sociology's Institutionalism". *International Organization*, vol. 50, no. 2, pp. 325–47

Florini, Ann. 1996. "The Evolution of International Norms". *International Studies Quarterly*, vol. 40, pp. 363–89.

Freeman, Edward Augustus. 1891. *The History of Sicily from the Earliest Times*, Volume 1. Oxford: Clarendon Press.

Gifford, Julie A. 2011. *Buddhist Practice and Visual Culture: The Visual Rhetoric of Borobudur*. Abingdon: Routledge.

Goldstein, Judith. 1993. *Ideas, Interests, and American Trade Policy*. Ithaca: Cornell University Press.

Goldstein, Judith and Robert O. Keohane. 1993. "Ideas and Foreign Policy: An Analytic Framework". In *Ideas and Foreign Policy: Beliefs, Institutions, and Political Change*, edited by Judith Goldstein and Robert O. Keohane. Ithaca: Cornell University Press.

Gonda, Jan. 1952. *Sanskrit in Indonesia*. Nagpur: International Academy of Indian Culture.

———. 1973. *Sanskrit in Indonesia* (2nd Edition). Nagpur: International Academy of Indian Culture.

Groslier, B.P. 1960. "Our Knowledge of Khmer Civilization: A Reappraisal". *Journal of the Siam Society*, vol. 49, no. 1, pp. 1–28.

Hall, D.G.E. 1960. "Looking at Southeast Asian History". *Journal of Asian Studies*, vol. 19, no. 3, pp. 243–53.

———. 1981. *A History of South-East Asia* (4th Edition). New York: St. Martin's Press.

Heine-Geldern, Robert. 1956. Conceptions of State and Kingship in Southeast Asia. Data Paper: Number 18, Southeast Asia Program, Cornell University, Ithaca, New York, April 1953.

Heine-Geldern, Robert. 1942. "Conceptions of State and Kingship in Southeast Asia". *Far Eastern Quarterly*, vol. 2, no. 1, pp. 15–30.

Hernandez, Carolina. 1995. *ASEAN Perspectives on Human Rights and Democracy in International Relations: Problems and Prospects*. Working Paper. Centre for International Studies: University of Toronto.

Hodos, Tamar. 2006. *Local Responses to Colonization in the Iron Age Mediterranean*. London/New York: Routledge.

Hooker, M.B. 1978. *A Concise Legal History of South-East Asia*, Oxford: Clarendon Press.

Hooykaas, Christiaan. 1973. *Religion in Bali*. Leiden: Brill.

Huntington, Samuel P. 1993. "The Clash of Civilizations?". *Foreign Affairs*, vol. 72, no. 3 (Summer), pp. 22–49

———. 1996. *The Clash of Civilizations and the Remaking of World Order*. New York: Simon & Schuster.

Jannelli, Lorena, and Fausto Longo. 2004. *The Greeks in Sicily*. Verona: Arsenale Editrice.

Katzenstein, Peter J., ed. 1996. *The Culture of National Security: Norms and Identity in World Politics*. New York: Columbia University Press.

———. ed. 2010. "A World of Plural and Pluralist Civilizations". In *Civilizations in World Politics*. New York: Routledge.

———. ed. 2010. *Civilizations in World Politics*. New York: Routledge.

Katzenstein, Peter, Robert O. Keohane and Stephen D. Krasner. 1999. "International Organization and the Study of World Politics". *International Organization*, vol. 52, no. 4, pp. 645–85.

Keohane, Robert O. 1984. *After Hegemony: Cooperation and Discord in the World Political Economy*. Princeton: Princeton University Press.

Keyes, Charles F. 1992. "A Conference at Wingspread and Rethinking Southeast Asian Studies". In *Southeast Asian Studies in Balance: Reflections from America*, edited by Charles Hirschman, Charles F. Keyes and Karl Hutterer. Ann Arbor, Michigan: Association for Asian Studies, pp. 9–24.

Kirsch, Thomas A. 1977. "Complexity in the Thai Religious System". *Journal of Asian Studies*, vol. 36, no. 2, pp. 241–66.

Klotz, Audie. 1995*a*. "Norms Reconstituting Interests: global racial equality and U.S. Sanctions against South Africa". *International Organization*, vol. 49, no. 3, pp. 451–78

————. 1995*b. Norms in International Relations: The Struggle Against Apartheid.* Ithaca: Cornell University Press.

Knappert, Jan. 1999. *Myths and Folklore in South-east Asia.* Kuala Lumpur: Oxford University Press.

Krause, Keith. 2001. Norm-Building in Security Spaces: The Emergence of the Light Weapons Problematic, Working Paper 11, Montreal, Research Group in International Security, Joint Program of the Universite de Montreal and McGill University.

Kulke, Hermann. 2011. Indian Colonies, Indianization or Cultural Convergence? Reflections on the Changing Image of India's Role in Southeast Asia. Paper presented to the conference on "Asian Encounters: Networks of Cultural Interactions," University of Delhi, India, 30 October–4 November 2011.

————. 1993. Max Weber's Contribution to the Study of 'Hinduization' in India and 'Indianization' in Southeast Asia. In *Kings and Cults: State Formation and Legitimation in India*, edited by Hermann Kulke. New Delhi: Manohar, pp. 240–61.

Legge, John. 1992. The Writing of Southeast Asian History. In *The Cambridge History of Southeast Asia*, edited by Tarling, Nicholas. Cambridge: Cambridge University Press, pp. 1–50.

Litfin, Karen. 1994. *Ozone Discourses: Science and Politics in Global Environmental Cooperation.* New York: Columbia University Press.

Lumsdaine, David. 1993. *Moral Vision in International Politics.* Princeton: Princeton University Press.

Mabbett, I.W. 1976. "The 'Indianization' of Southeast Asia: Reflections on the Prehistoric Sources". *Journal of Southeast Asian Studies*, vol. 8, no. 1, pp. 1–14.

————. 1976. "The 'Indianization' of Southeast Asia: Reflections on the Historical Sources". *Journal of Southeast Asian Studies*, vol. 8, no. 2, pp. 143–61.

Majumdar, R.C. 1948. *Greater India* (2nd Edition), Bombay: National Information and Publications.

Majumdar, R.C., H.C. Raychaudhuri, and Kalikinkar Datta. 1948. *An Advanced History of India.* London: Macmillan and Co. Ltd.

Manguin, Pierre-Yves. 2011. Introduction. In *Early Interactions between South and Southeast Asia*, edited by Pierre-Yves Manguin, A. Mani, and Geoff Wade. Singapore: Institute of Southeast Asian Studies.

Maxwell, T.S. 2007. Religion at the Time of Jayavarman VII. In *Bayon: New Perspectives*, edited by Joyce Clark. Bangkok: River Books, pp. 72–135.

McElroy, Robert. 1992. *Morality and American Foreign Policy*. Princeton: Princeton University Press.

Munslow, Alun. 2000. *The Routledge Companion to Historical Studies*. London: Routledge.

Muller, Harald. 1993. The Internalization of Principles, Norms, and Rules by Governments: The Case of Security Regimes. In *Regime Theory and International Relations*, edited by Volker Rittberger. Oxford: Oxford University Press, pp. 361–88.

Nadelmann, Ethan. 1990. "Global Prohibition Regimes: The Evolution of Norms in International Society". *International Organization*, vol. 44, pp. 479–524.

O'Connor, Stanley J. 1986. *The Archaeology of Peninsular Siam*. Bangkok: The Siam Society.

Olivia, Pavel. 1981. *The Birth of Greek Civilization*. London: Book Club Associates.

O'Reilly, Dougald J.W. 2007. *Early Civilizations of Southeast Asia*. Lanham: Rowman and Littlefield.

Osborne, Milton. 1979. *Southeast Asia: An Introductory History*. Sydney: Allen & Unwin.

Parsons, Talcott. 1996. *Societies: Comparative and Evolutionary Perspectives* Englewood Cliffs: Prentice Hall.

Patra, Benudhar. 2010. *Role of Kalinga in the Process of Ancient Indian Colonization in South-East Asia*. Orissa Review, pp. 17–28.

Peterson, M.J. 1992. "Whales, Cetologists, Environmentalists and the International Management of Whaling". *International Organization*, vol. 46, no. 1 (Winter), pp. 147–86.

Pollock, Sheldon. 1996. The Sanskrit Cosmopolis, 300–1300: Transculturation, Vernacularization, and the Question of Ideology. In *Ideology and Status of Sanskrit*, edited by Jan E.M Houben. Leiden: E.J. Brill, pp. 197–247.

Pollock, Sheldon. 2006. *The Language of the Gods in the World of Men: Sanskrit, Culture and Power in Premodern India*. Chicago: University of Chicago Press.

Price, Richard. 1997. *The Chemical Weapons Taboo*. Ithaca: Cornell University Press.

————. 1998. "Reversing the Gun Sights: Transnational Civil Society Targets Land Mines". *International Organization*, vol. 52, no. 3, pp. 613–44.

Price, Richard, and Nina Tamnenwald. 1996. Norms and Deterrence: The Nuclear and Chemical Weapons Taboos. In *The Culture of National Security*, edited by Peter Katzenstein. Ithaca: Cornell University Press, pp. 114–52.

Risse, Thomas. 2000. "Rational Choice, Constructivism, and the Study of International Institutions", Paper Presented at the Annual Meeting of the American Political Science Association, Washington, D.C., 31 August–3 September 2000.

Risse, Thomas, Stephen C. Ropp, and Kathryn Sikkink (eds.). 1999. *The Power of Human Rights: International Norms and Domestic Change.* Cambridge, UK, and New York: Cambridge University Press.

Sardesai, D.R. 1994. *Southeast Asia: Past and Present* (3rd Edition). Boulder, Co. Westview Press.

Sen, Tansen. 2009. The Military Campaigns of Rajendra Chola and the Chola-Srivijaya-China Triangle. In *Nagapattinam to Suvarnadwipa: Reflections on Chola Naval Expeditions to Southeast Asia*, edited by Hermann Kulke, K. Kesavapany and Vijay Sakhuja. Singapore: Institute of Southeast Asian Studies, pp. 61–75.

Sikkink, Kathryn. 1993. The Power of Principled Ideas: Human Rights Policies in the United States and Latin America. In *Ideas and Foreign Policy*, edited by Goldstein, Judith and Robert Keohane. Ithaca. Cornell University Press, pp. 138–70.

————. 1993. "Human Rights, Principled Issue Networks and Sovereignty in Latin America". *International Organization*, vol. 47, no. 3, pp. 411–41.

Snidal, Duncan. 1985. "The Limits of Hegemonic Stability Theory". *International Organization*, vol. 39, (Autumn), pp. 579–614.

Roberts, John (ed.) 2007. *Oxford Dictionary of the Classical World*. Oxford: Oxford University Press.

Smail, John R. 1961. "On the Possibility of an Autonomous History of Modern Southeast Asia". *Journal of Southeast Asian History*, vol. 2, no. 2, pp. 72–102.

Solheim, Wilhelm. 1971. "New Light on a Forgotten Past". *National Geographic*, vol. 139, no. 3, pp. 330–39.

Tambiah, Stanley J. 1976. *World Conqueror and World Renouncer: A Study of Buddhism and Polity in Thailand against a Historical Background.* Cambridge: Cambridge University Press.

Thapar, Romila. 1996. *Ashoka and the Decline of the Mauryas* (15th Edition). New Delhi: Oxford University Press.

Tilly, Charles. 1975. Reflections on the History of European State-Making. In *The Formation of National States in Western Europe*, edited by Charles Tilly. Princeton: Princeton University Press, pp. 3–83.

Van Der Kroeff, Justus M. 1951. "The Hinduization of Indonesia Reconsidered". *Far Eatsern Quarterly*, vol. 9, no. 1, pp. 17–30.

Van Leur, J.C. 1955. On Early Asian Trade. In *Indonesian Trade and Society: Essays in Asian Social and Economic History*, edited by J.C. Van Leur. The Hague: W.van Hoeve Ltd.

Wales, H.G. Quaritch. 1951. *The Making of Greater India*. London: Bernard Quaritch (2nd Edition 1961, 3rd Edition 1974).

Weber, Max. 1958. *The Religion of India: Sociology of Hinduism and Buddhism.* Translated by Hans Gerth and Don Martindale, Glencoe. The Free Press.

Wendt, Alexander. 1999. *Social Theory of International Politics.* Cambridge: Cambridge University Press

Wertheim, W.F. 1954. "Early Asian Trade: An Appreciation of J.C. van Leur". *Far Eastern Quarterly*, vol. 13, no. 2, pp. 167–73.

Wheatley, Paul. 1964. Desultory Remarks on the Ancient History of the Malay Peninsula. In *Malayan and Indonesian Studies*, edited by John Bastin and R. Roolvink. Oxford: Oxford University Press, pp. 33–75.

———. 1973. Comments on the Dynamics of the Process of Indianization. In *Early Malaysia: Some observations on the nature of Indian contacts with pre-British Malaya*, edited by K.S. Sandhu. Singapore: University Education Press, pp. 37–49.

———. 1982. "Presidential Address: India Beyond the Ganges — Desultory Reflections on the Origins of Civilization in Southeast Asia". *Journal of Asian Studies*, vol. 42, no. 1, pp. 13–28.

Wertheim, W.F. 1956. *Indonesian Society in Transition (A Study of Social Change)*. The Hague: W. Van Hoeve Ltd.

Wolters, O.W. 1982. *History, Culture and Region in Southeast Asian Perspectives.* Singapore: Institute of Southeast Asian Studies (2nd Edition 1999).

INDEX

Titles in the Nalanda-Sriwijaya Research Series

Series Editor: Tansen Sen

1. *Preserving Cultural Identity through Education: The Schools of the Chinese Community in Calcutta, India,* by Zhang Xing

2. *Civilizations in Embrace: The Spread of Ideas and the Transformation of Power; India and Southeast Asia in the Classical Age,* by Amitav Acharya

www.ingramcontent.com/pod-product-compliance
Lightning Source LLC
Chambersburg PA
CBHW060346100426
42812CB00003B/1147